SUICIDE

SUICIDE

- *Prevention*
- *Intervention*
- *Postvention*

SECOND EDITION
Updated and Expanded

Earl A. Grollman

BEACON PRESS ▸ BOSTON

Beacon Press
25 Beacon Street
Boston, Massachusetts 02108

Beacon Press books
are published under the auspices of
the Unitarian Universalist Association
of Congregations.

95   94   93   92   91   90   8   7   6   5   4

Text design by Copenhaver Cumpston

Library of Congress Cataloging-in-Publication Data

Grollman, Earl A.
   Suicide: prevention, intervention, postvention.
   Bibliography: p.
   1. Suicide.   2. Euthanasia.   3. Suicide—United States
—Prevention—Directories.   I. Title.
HV6545.G7   1988   362.2   87-47880
ISBN 0-8070-2707-3

▸ Contents

1 ▸ Suicide: The Problem   1

*Suicide Could Happen to You; Incidence; What Is Suicide?;
Indirect Suicide; Autocide; Alcoholism; Drug Abuse; Other
Forms of Subintentioned Suicide*

2 ▸ Views on Suicide throughout History   13

*Egyptian, Greek, Roman, and Later Cultures; Judaism;
Christianity; Islam; Japanese Religious Faiths; Critique*

3 ▸ Suicide: The Theorists   27

*Sigmund Freud; Karl Menninger; Alfred Adler; Carl Jung;
James Hillman; Harry Stack Sullivan; Karen Horney; Emile
Durkheim; Norman L. Faberow; Edwin S. Schneidman; A.
Alvarez; Elisabeth Kübler-Ross*

4 ▸ Suicide: The Social Context   35

*Economic Conditions; Occupation; Male and Female; Mari-
tal Status; Youth; Middle Age; The Elderly; Cities and
Neighborhoods; Race; Geography; War and Peace; Time of
Year; Media and Cluster Suicides; Jail Suicides; Homosex-
uals; Religion*

5 ▸ Clues to Suicide: Prevention   62

The Suicide Attempt; The Suicide Threat; The Situational Hint; The Family Hint; The Emotional Hint; Behavioral Hints; Mental Illness; Those Most Susceptible to Suicide

6 ▸ Helping the Potential Suicide: Intervention   76

The Attitude of the Helper; The Helper as Moralizer; What You Can Do to Help

7 ▸ When Suicide Is Committed: Postvention   88

The Grieving Process; Accept Your Grief; When to Seek Professional Help; The Funeral; Children Grieve, Too; Recovering from Grief; Helping Survivor-Victims; Withdrawal and Return

8 ▸ Euthanasia: Killing and Letting Die   105

Euthanasia: What It Is; The Living Will; Passive Euthanasia; Active Euthanasia; The Right to Suicide

9 ▸ A Summons for Community Action   112

Making Death Come Alive; Making Suicide More Understandable; The Suicide Prevention Center; Help for Families of Suicide

▸ Conclusion   123

▸ Appendix   125

For More Information; Suicide Prevention/Crisis Intervention Centers in the United States

▸ Bibliography   145

1 ▸ *Suicide:*
The Problem

Suicide is a whispered word, inappropriate for polite company. Family and friends often pretend they do not hear the word's dread sound even when it is uttered. For suicide is a taboo subject that stigmatizes not only the victim but the survivors as well.

Of course, any natural death has its share of emotional repercussions: loneliness, disbelief, heartache, and torment. With self-inflicted death, the emotions are intensified to unbelievable and unbearable proportions. People with suicidal intentions are under intense mental strain which they feel incapable of resolving. If they succeed in taking their life, those left behind experience not only the pain of separation but aggravated feelings of guilt, shame, anger, and self-blame. The act of self-destruction raises the obvious questions "Why?" and "What could I have done to prevent it?" Anxious and grief-stricken, each survivor asks: "How can I face my friends? What will they think of me?" Death is a robber. Death by suicide, however, represents the greatest of all affronts to those who remain. As Dr. Edwin S. Schneidman, the famous suicidologist said: "The suicidal person places his [or her] psychological skeleton in the survivor's closet."

Until recently, the twentieth-century person thought of suicide as a private matter. Even many physicians believed that individuals were entitled to die as they wished. To most, self-imposed death was some bizarre form of unconventional behavior, which usually signified insanity. Today, with a greater awareness of the increasing complexity of human life, we must acknowledge that suicide is more than just a personal decision; it is a disease of civilization. The iron curtain of silence must be lifted!

The purpose of this book is both to remove ancient myths and to review the recent studies that have broadened our knowledge of this human dilemma. What can we do for the *prevention* of suicide, to achieve a clearer understanding before the horrible fact? What can we do for the *intervention* of suicide, to enter into helpful communication during the overwhelming crisis? And finally, what can we do for the *postvention* of suicide, to provide meaningful support for those who have experienced the intolerable loss of a loved one through self-inflicted death?

The philosopher George Santayana once said: "That life is worth living is the most necessary of assumptions, and were it not assumed, the most impossible of conclusions."

▶ Suicide Could Happen to You

Almost everybody at one time or another contemplates suicide. Self-destruction is one of many choices open to human beings. Dr. Joost Meerloo, author of *Suicide and Mass Suicide*, declared: "Eighty per cent of people admit to having 'played' with suicidal ideas." And the medical statistician Louis I. Dublin told an astonished audience of physicians in Los Angeles:

It would not be rash to estimate that perhaps as many as two million individuals are now living in our country who have a history of at least one unsuccessful attempt at self-execution. A great many of these will try again. On the basis of a recent study, ten percent will ultimately succeed. This fact must be emphasized in order to impress the huge size of the problem with which we are involved and to focus attention on the need for a more concerted effort on the part of socially oriented groups to attack this problem seriously.

No single group, race, or class of people is free from the "unpardonable sin of society." Though a person may never utter the word "suicide," does this mean that she or he is totally free of death wishes? Everyone has a tendency to self-destruction which varies in degree of intensity from individual to individual and from one society to another. Psychologists find that the wish to die is frequent among children and that suicidal fantasies are common in normal adults.

These suicidal wishes can be expressed in different ways:

"If I died now, my parents would be sorry for being so mean to me."

"I would rather die than go on living this way."

"I'm tired of life."

"You would be better off without me."

"I won't be around much longer for you to put up with."

If these expressions seem to the casual observer to be unrelated to suicide, it must be emphasized that these precise words are the verbal sentiments expressed in presuicidal communications and conversations.

Threats can turn into action. In place of a passive acceptance of unmanageable difficulties comes an active declaration of independence—self-imposed death. It is as if the victim cries out: "At least I am competent to do this!"

▶ Incidence

Once every minute someone tries to kill him- or herself with conscious intent. Sixty or seventy times a day these attempts succeed. Each year in the United States alone some 25,800 reported persons take their own lives.

Unquestionably the number is even higher, since the true cause of death is often unreported or masked under labels like "accidental death." Some believe that the actual statistics could be as high as 100,000. According to Gregory Zilboorg, former psychiatrist-in-chief of the United Nations: "Statistical data on suicide as compiled today deserves little credence. All too many suicides are not reported as such."

What constitutes suicide in one county, city, or state is often not the same in a neighboring area, for the coroner, who may be an elected political official and not a physician, would prefer to list other, more acceptable causes of death.

To many people, suicide is an affront to God, the family, community, and society, and few experts doubt that many unnatural deaths are covered up. A police chief in a local town admitted, "If a man hangs himself, we just cut him down, rush the dead body to the hospital, and enter some other malady as the cause of death. This way we spare the family the terrible disgrace." The true American suicide rate may be two to three times the reported statistics.

The problem is getting worse. There is a marked increase in the number of attempts and deaths by young people aged fifteen to twenty-four. Prior to the late 1960s, that group made up a relatively negligible number of total suicides. Since 1960, suicide among adolescents has increased 265 percent.

It is estimated that there are approximately 100 suicide attempts for every completed suicide. Every year, 10,000 older Americans kill themselves. Although the aged comprise 11 percent of the population, they account for 25 percent of the reported suicides.

Suicide, which once ranked twenty-second on the list of causes of death in the United States, now rates ninth, and in some states, sixth. Today, the toll is greater than the combined deaths from typhoid fever, dysentery, scarlet fever, diptheria, whooping cough, meningococcal infections, infantile paralysis, measles, typhus, malaria, bronchitis, and rheumatic fever.

The number of suicides is grossly underreported for a number of reasons. Families are reluctant to have the death pronounced a suicide, not only because of the social stigma attached, but also because of the possible loss of life insurance benefits, since many policies do not pay face value under these circumstances. Equally important is the fact that authorities do not always agree upon the manner of death.

▶ What Is Suicide?

A young man is found dead with a bullet between his eyes. Beside him is a rifle he has had for a year, with equipment for cleaning it. Accident or suicide?

To be classified a suicide, a person must intend to kill him- or herself and must actually do so. This is easier to claim than to prove. Did the youth in the above incident intend to take his life? What about Marilyn Monroe, with her overdose of sleeping pills? Was this an intentional death?

One way to determine intention is through psychological autopsy. Edwin Schneidman asserts that a team of social scientists must first interview all the people who were close to the victim and record every reaction and recollection while the memories are still fresh. "The investigators would know things about the person that many people close to him did not know about him. And they would find out things about him that he did not know about himself!" The interviewers would then record the type of death on the certificate using one of the letters N, A, S, or H, which stand for *N*atural death, *A*ccidental death, *S*uicide, or *H*omocide.

▶ Indirect Suicide

There are those who are suicidal and yet are not recognized as such by family, friends, and uninformed professionals. Desperate people may find life intolerable and unmanageable and thus engage in death-oriented behavior. In 1897, Emile Durkheim labeled this "symbolic suicide." Karl Menninger called it "chronic suicide" with "indirect self-destructive behavior that undermines one's own health." N. B. Tabachnik defines self-destructive behavior as "any activity over which one has some (actual or potential) volitional control which moves him or her in the direction of an earlier physical death than would otherwise occur." Life-shortening behavior has also been designated as a "partial, a subintentional, a submeditated suicide," a "hidden suicide," "unconscious suicidal behavior," or "suicide equivalent."

People may kill themselves slowly without being consciously aware of their lethal intentions. The individuals involved would deny that their actions are meant to destroy or injure themselves. Yet their entire life-style involves a movement toward the brink of self-destruction. The same psychic forces that impel an individual to jump from a skyscraper may be responsible for such dangerous habits as heavy abuse of alcohol and/or drugs, ignoring serious illness, overeating, overworking, or chronic smoking.

Calvin J. Frederick of the National Institute of Mental Health cites seven prominent characteristics of indirect suicide:

> (1) There is often a lack of full awareness of the consequences, (2) the behavior is rationalized, intellectualized, or denied, (3) the onset could be gradual but death is precipitous, (4) open discussion seldom occurs, (5) long suffering, martyrlike

behavior may appear, (6) secondary gain is obtained by evoking sympathy and/or expressing hostility via the process, and (7) death is most often seen as accidental.

Even though indirect suicide is less obvious, the results are just as deadly.

▶ Autocide

One place to look out for disguised suicides is on the road. The car is an ideal instrument of self-annihilation. The popular wisdom that exclaims as a car shoots past at an excessive speed, "Man, he's trying to kill himself!" could in many cases be correct. Many deaths reported as accidents are frequently disguised suicides. Police officers often use the term "autocide" for fatal accidents when a vehicle is used as a method of self-imposed death. Elevated blood alcohol levels are found in 40 percent of victims of fatal traffic accidents. It is debatable as to how "accidental" these accidents really are.

Authorities have postulated that inattentiveness, excessive speed, errors in judgment, and driving while under the influence of alcohol and/or drugs are often the products of conscious or unconscious self-destructive behavior. In a study by the Los Angeles Suicide Prevention Center, researchers found that 25 percent of the accident victims they studied were depressed people with feelings of helplessness typical of suicidal individuals. Before their accident, they recounted fantasies of death and self-destruction. An educated guess is that one-quarter of drivers who die in auto accidents cause them intentionally or subintentionally by imprudent and excessive risk-taking.

Traffic accidents are especially high among adolescents. Each year more than 19,000 teenagers and young adults die in automobile mishaps. Dartmouth Medical School psychiatrists studied the driving records and family lives of 496 teenagers aged 16 to 19 in New Hampshire. They stated that

the males most likely to have accidents were outgoing, bois-
terous, rebellious people with a strong "macho" image. Under stress they turned to drink or drugs and then drove
carelessly and impulsively with more interest in power and
speed than safety. On the whole, females were considered
safer drivers. It is believed that they can more easily express
their inner feelings than the males who behave in a so-called
masculine way.

Automobile accidents cause enormous human suffering
and economic loss for victims, their families, and society as
a whole. From the point of view of prevention, it is of great
importance to discern the underlying motivations of the
unsafe drivers. The Federal Center for Studies of Suicide
Prevention in Bethesda, Maryland, confirms that many drivers play latent unconscious roles in hastening their own
deaths. They kill not only themselves but innocent people
as well. The use of a car as a method of self-destruction is
peculiarly resistant to later observation, statistics, and analysis. People who attempt autocide rarely leave suicide notes.

▶ Alcoholism

There is an extremely high suicide risk among alcoholics.
Alcoholism is associated with 20 to 30 percent of the general
suicides; among young people it may be as high as 50 percent or more. Prolonged drinking induces progressive
depression, guilt, and psychic pain, which are known frequently to precede suicide.

Alcohol abusers frequently feel deprived of love. They
utilize alcohol to dull their pain. Since alcohol is a depres-
sant, the initial high they experience at first fades quickly.
They then feel even more depressed and guilty for being
inebriated. A cycle is thus created—depression leading to
drinking, leading to more depression, leading to ever more
frequent bouts of drunkenness.

As a result, there is the loss of family, friends, and
employment. Studies show that many alcoholics who take

their lives experience the loss of a close relationship within six weeks preceding the suicide. An alcoholic individual is at especially high risk during interpersonal crisis. Alcohol deepens aggressiveness, which can lead to self-destruction when turned against oneself.

Alcoholics may not consciously kill themselves but their chronic drinking is a form of life-shortening activity. The toxic effects of alcohol on every organ system of the body are well known and documented throughout the scientific literature. Severe physical deterioration and malnutrition accompany the alcoholic life-style. When death occurs, it may not be listed as "suicide" but as due to a physical cause such as cirrhosis. But whether it is the deterioration of relationships caused by alcoholism, or the intrinsic effects of alcohol on physical or emotional well-being, or, most likely, some combination of all of these, there is little doubt that alcoholism is a significant factor in the suicidal syndrome.

▶ Drug Abuse

Alcohol is often combined either suicidally or accidentally with barbiturates, tranquilizers, or heroin. Drugs and alcohol represent a particularly lethal combination. They impair impulse control and exacerbate depression or even psychosis.

Drug abuse and suicide are closely allied. The chronic ingestion and effects of controlled substances as well as the general life-style of the substance abusers are to a significant degree directed toward self-destruction, irrespective of conscious intent. Psychologists have observed the relationship between multi-drug abuse and feelings of depression and anxiety. In a psychoanalytic study of this phenomenon as early as 1933, S. Rado coined the term "pharmacothymia" to describe the disorder in which drugs are taken to find surcease from intolerable psychic pain. He stressed that drugs were perceived to have magical qualities which could afford a sense of heightened self-esteem and help alleviate melancholy moods.

As with alcoholics, the toxic effects of the ingested drugs predispose the abuser to a wide range of ailments and diseases. Addicts are more prone to develop serious illnesses such as hepatitis and endocarditis, which result for the most part from contaminated drugs or syringes, and also suffer from a life-style that frequently involves exposure to the elements and malnutrition.

Addicts are also more likely to contract the fatal disease AIDS. AIDS stands for *A*cquired *I*mmune *D*eficiency *Syn*drome and is caused by a special virus called a "retrovirus" that invades crucial immune cells and destroys them. Approximately 17 percent of those at risk for AIDS are IV (intravenous) drugs abusers. The AIDS virus lives in the blood cells taken up in the syringes and is spread when needles are shared. The estimate is that 1.3 million to 2.7 million Americans will die of AIDS by 1991.

A recent study of drug abusers in large American cities has substantiated the belief that drugs are currently a major means of committing suicide. Not only the young but the aged as well kill themselves with overdoses of medicines. The leading generic drugs listed as being used in elderly suicide are as follows: pentabarbital, 38.3 percent; secobarbital, 26.6 percent; phenobarbital, 6.9 percent; salicylate, 5.8 percent; and seco/amobarbital, 5.1 percent.

Many drug abusers and potential suicides—both young and old—feel unloved and unloving. As psychiatrist Isidor Sadger comments, "Nobody commits suicide who has not given up hope for love." Drugs dull feelings and keep family, friends, and the world at a distance. Some alternate between taking drugs and attempting suicide.

▶ Other Forms of Subintentioned Suicide

As usually defined, suicide is the deliberate taking of one's life. It has become apparent that there is a larger number of people who want to die, but have not reached that state where they will act consciously on a suicidal desire.

Accident-type suicides are not as rare as the casual observer might believe. Those who are accident-prone may believe they are careful, yet they behave in curiously self-destructive ways, such as stabbing themselves with a knife or "accidentally" taking too many sleeping pills.

Some people are not sure they wish to die, nor are they convinced that they want to live. This ambivalence is demonstrated in deadly "games" reminiscent of Russian roulette. By leaving the outcome of such "games" to external forces (which take the place of the bullet in the gun), the decision is made for them. A gamble with death is also involved in other daredevil feats, such as auto racing and parachute jumping.

A suicide equivalent may be camouflaged in idealistic and altruistic garb. Martyrs may give up their lives for the honor of God and country. Unconsciously, they may wish to die. Then an opportunity arises that allows them to do so with honor and nobility. By their intrepid bravery, they gain our gratitude, not our disdain.

In some cultures, the act of taking one's life is considered heroic. In India, a Hindu widow is forbidden by law to throw herself on the funeral pyre of her husband but at one time this was the custom among women of the upper castes. There are the idealistic people who take violent actions in the cause of nonviolence for an allegedly greater good. One can recall viewing on television the Buddhist monks who bathed in gasoline, ignited themselves, and calmly burned to death in their dramatic effort to protest what they considered to be an immoral war in Southeast Asia.

Many deaths are not ruled as suicides even though definite unconscious lethal intention is involved. To clarify the situation, the Suicide Prevention Center of Los Angeles proposed three workable psychological classifications for cause of death. An *unintended* death is one in which individuals play no active role in their own demise. An *intentional* death is one in which the victims have an active part in their own death through deliberate or impulsive acts. In the *subintentional* death the victims play a partial, unconscious, covert role in their own self-destruction.

There are many ways of committing suicide besides slashing one's wrists, or swallowing poison, or shooting or hanging oneself. Suicide, by any name, is the number one cause of unnecessary deaths. And in the words of Justice Cardoza, "A cry for help is a summons for rescue."

2 ▶ *Views on Suicide throughout History*

▶ Egyptian, Greek, Roman, and Later Cultures

People have been killing themselves since the beginning of recorded history. Attitudes toward suicide vary from age to age and from civilization to civilization.

The First Egyptian Period (Seventh to Tenth Dynasty, ca. 2000 B.C.) has yielded the famous dialogue of a man with his soul in a debate about whether or not to kill himself. The man states that his existence is filled with unendurable pain and suffering, and he seriously contemplates taking his life without showing any hint of religious fear. The ancient Egyptians did not consider suicide to be a violation of their spiritual or legal code.

Stoicism, the school of philosophy founded at Athens about 300 B.C., believed in leading "life according to nature." When circumstances made existence no longer bearable, one could voluntarily withdraw from life by suicide. A Roman Stoic who believed that he had "had enough of life" had his veins severed by trained technicians. Marcus Porcius Cato (95 B.C.–46 B.C.), a renowned Stoic philosopher, loathed life under Caesar's despotism and decided to com-

13

mit suicide. After dinner, during which he talked about philosophy, he retired to his room, read Plato's discussion of immortality in the *Phaedo,* and then stabbed himself. His friends rushed to his assistance and dressed his wounds. Cato removed the bandages, extracted his intestines, and then died.

Epicureans also believed that the suicide was an acceptable choice. As a philosophical doctrine, Epicureanism had its rise in the teaching of its founder, Epicurus, who was born in the year 341 B.C. in Samos, an island in the Aegean Sea forty-five miles south of Smyrna and died in Athens in 270 B.C. According to his theory of life, a person's primary goal is the attainment of pleasure for a tranquil and happy mind. When life no longer affords happiness, suicide becomes a viable alternative. "Death is nothing to us, because when we are, death is not; when death is, we are not."

There were dissenters who condemned suicidal acts. Plato (427 B.C.–347 B.C.) derided the Epicurean doctrine. In his *Republic,* Plato's ethical theory defines justice as the right to grasp available pleasure. "Only one thing I know," he wrote, speaking through the mouth of Socrates, "that it is better, if need be, to suffer the extreme of injustice." The function of reason is to furnish true principles of conduct to the individual—to provide courage even amid a life of affliction and lamentation.

The Greek philosopher Socrates, also born in Athens (469 B.C.–399 B.C.), argued that suicide was *never* morally justified. He asserted that human beings, the property of the gods, had no right to do away with that which does not belong to them. Variations of this argument ascribing control over death to the gods, or to the one God, have become the most pervasive justification for maintaining that suicide is immoral. The poets Virgil (70 B.C.–19 B.C.) and Ovid (43 B.C.–A.D. 18) concurred that taking one's life could never be condoned.

With the passage of time, society began to react in a hostile manner (with some noticeable exceptions) against self-inflicted death. Some thinkers asserted that the manner in which a person departs from life reflects not only one's own philosophy of life but a possible contempt for the group as well. The theologian Thomas Aquinas (A.D. 1225–74) argued that suicide robbed the community of one of its integral parts. An individual had the duty to live even against his or her own wishes because of obligations to the group. The German philosopher Immanuel Kant (1788) summed it up: "Suicide is an insult to humanity." How different from the earlier Roman philosopher Lucius Seneca (4 B.C.–A.D. 65) in his Epistle 70: "The wise man will live as long as he ought, not as long as he can. . . . It is not a question of dying earlier or later, but dying well or ill. And dying well means escape from the danger of living ill."

Suicide came to be regarded as taboo within the religious tradition enunciated by Flavius Josephus (ca. A.D. 37–100), one of the great Jewish historians. (These sentiments were later echoed in the daughter religions, Christianity and Islam.) The ancient Israelites were intensely concerned for the survival of their tiny nomadic group, and regarded the suicide of even one Hebrew as a threat to tribal continuity. Other faiths considered suicide to be a rejection of both God and the promise of an eternal life.

The custom arose of burying suicides at a crossroads as a token of disgrace. Indignities were practiced on the corpse: the body was dragged through the streets, a stake was driven through the heart, and the dead person was left for carrion birds to destroy. Superstitions grew up about the suicide's ghost. If a pregnant woman stepped on the grave of a suicide, it was said, her child would eventually die in a self-destructive way.

Theological restrictions were translated into both criminal and civil laws. Early English practice penalized survivors by confiscating their property. In the sixteenth century, a person who persuaded another to kill him- or herself was guilty of murder. The doctrine of "blameworthy intent" equated suicide with homicide. In 1829 burial in the highway was ended in England by a parliamentary act which directed that burial be in churchyards or other burial places, but *without* religious ceremony and between 9:00 P.M. and midnight.

Suicide was a felony in England and other countries. The punishment for an attempted suicide was imprisonment. Sir William Blackstone, the distinguished English jurist (1723–80) considered suicide to be a double curse— against both the king and God. Statutes were enacted against suicide attempters as well as the survivors as a form of chastisement and as a deterrent for future attempters.

Yet it was discovered that the courts had no ability to prevent people from taking their life upon release. Therefore, after 1916, instead of being imprisoned, the individual was placed in the custody of relatives and friends. It was not until 1961 that the British Parliament enacted a bill abolishing the criminality of suicide. For the first time in a thousand years the act of suicide was not considered "a species of felony."

In recent years, legal restrictions have been abolished in almost every country. In the United States, various states have had varying opinions on the criminality of suicide. Illinois stated that it "had never regarded the English laws as to suicide as applicable to the spirit of our institutions." New York considered suicide a "grave public wrong" but not a crime. In 1937, a New Jersey court declared that an attempted suicide was an indictable offense punishable by imprisonment not exceeding three years and a fine not more than $1,000 or both. Thirty-five years later, a New Jersey statute terminated possible prosecution for attempted suicides. South Carolina, Alabama, and Massachusetts considered attempted suicide to be a crime but, of course, not punishable if accomplished.

In 1968, the American Medical Association commented: "Where a state by statute provides that attempted suicide is a misdemeanor . . . since no penalty is attached . . . the misdemeanor of attempted suicide cannot be legally created." With new research in mental health, legislation has gradually but radically changed. Religion has been especially instrumental in the revoking of antisuicide statutes, for suicide laws in the United States were based on English common law, which was in turn profoundly influenced by the church and the synagogue.

▶ Judaism

"And God saw all that He had made, and found it very good." With almost the first words of Genesis, a thesis is stated that has echoed throughout the centuries: *life is good*; each person should treasure it and never despair of its possibilities, for behind it is God.

Despite a religious emphasis on the sanctity of life, the Hebrew Holy Scriptures contain but six brief references to self-destruction. In each case there are extenuating circumstances, such as the fear of being taken captive or the possibility of suffering humiliation or unbearable pain.

For example, Saul, the first king of Israel (1020 B.C.), was wounded by the Philistines. He called upon his armor bearer to slay him in order to prevent his being mocked and tortured by the enemy. Upon the frightened man's refusal, Saul fell upon his own sword.

In Flavius Josephus' *Antiquities of the Jews*, suicide is condoned as a mark of courage:

> And I have a good reason for such a discourse
> in the person of Saul, king of the Hebrews. For,
> although he knew what was coming upon him,
> and that he was to die immediately, by the pre-
> diction of the prophet, he determined not to flee

from death, nor from love of life to betray his
own people to the enemy, nor to bring disgrace
on his royal dignity, but exposing himself as well
as all his family and children to dangers, he
thought it a noble thing to fall together with
them, as he was fighting for his subjects, and
that it was better that his sons should die thus,
showing their courage, than to leave it uncertain
what they would be afterwards, for instead of
succession and posterity they gained commenda-
tion and a lasting name.

Later, Josephus was to condemn those who took their lives.

Three references to suicide are found in the books of
Maccabees (165 B.C.–A.D. 37). Each one relates to martyr-
dom. When capture by the Romans became inevitable, a
Jewish community in A.D. 73 committed mass suicide in the
fortress of Masada. Nine hundred and sixty persons killed
themselves along this western shore of the Red Sea rather
than fall into the hands of the enemy.

In Talmudic times (A.D. 200–500) an increasing number
of suicides is recorded. The rise is due partly to spiritual
and social crises, partly to a growing Greco-Roman influence. Now that the act had become more frequent, a
condemnatory tone was introduced. It was stated that self-
homicides forfeit their share in the world-to-come and shall
be denied burial honors. The Talmud decrees that suicides
are to receive no eulogy or public mourning, and they are
to be buried apart in community cemeteries.

There was not always universal agreement. Rabbi
Moses ben Nachman, the great Talmudist of the twelfth
century, asserted that relatives had a duty to the deceased
regardless of the circumstances of death. Other scholars
raised important queries concerning suicide: "How do you
know that the people really committed suicide, especially if
they had not explicitly declared their intent nor performed
the act in front of witnesses?" "If an individual was found

hanging on a tree, could it not have been an accidental death?" "Are the stringent rules valid for minors or the mentally incompetent?"

The Jewish sages realized that there were certain extenuating circumstances under which the rigid restrictions and prohibitions could be waived. Joseph Karo (1488–1575), perhaps the most outstanding of all the legal authorities, said: "Without proof to the contrary, a person is not pronounced to be wicked. If therefore an individual was discovered hanged or choked, as far as possible the act of killing should be regarded as the deed of another person and not his own deed." What about a minor? "If a minor committed suicide, it is considered that he had done the deed unwittingly." The matter was approached from the standpoint of mental illness: "If adults killed themselves and it is evident that the act was prompted by madness, they shall be treated as ordinary deceased people." Although considered a crime against God, suicide could sometimes be explained away, understood, and forgiven. In later years, many Jews committed suicide while in Nazi concentration camps waiting to be slaughtered. Controlling the time of their death was actually an affirmation of the victims' freedom.

In modern Judaism, there is both understanding and compassion concerning those who take their lives. Suicides are afforded all the honors and rites usually granted to the dead, thus sparing surviving relatives any further disgrace. Those who commit suicide are generally regarded as emotionally distressed and overwrought and therefore not responsible for their actions. Rabbi Yehiel Michel Epstein expressed these sentiments over eighty years ago in his influential code *Arukl Hashulchan:* "In regard to suicide we find *whatever* circumstances we can to remove the person who has apparently committed suicide from the denial of mourning rites."

In Judaism, suicide may be considered a violation of one of the Ten Commandments. The mystery of God-given life is still the most beautiful gift of all. However, with the

growth of the socio-psychological sciences, it has been realized that one cannot legislate against self-destruction by
religious fiat. Suicide must not be simply *condemned*. It must
be *understood* and *prevented*.

▶ Christianity

When Christianity came into being, suicide was very common in Greece and Rome. As mentioned, suicide was even
encouraged among the Stoics, the Cynics, the Cyrenaics,
and the Epicureans. The early Christians apparently ac-
cepted the prevailing attitudes of their era, particularly when
persecution made life unbearable. Many early Christians
submitted to Roman torture and allowed themselves to be
killed as martyrs. Suicides in this period, whether direct or
indirect, were based on the eagerness to do away with the
misery of the world in order to experience the joys of immortality. The Apostles did not denounce self-execution; the
New Testament touched on the question only indirectly, in
the report of Judas's death. For several centuries the leaders
of the church did not condemn this widespread practice.

Until Augustine (A.D. 354–430) denounced suicide as a
sin, there was no official church position against it. After
deliberating at great length whether self-imposed death
could be condoned in the case of a woman whose honor
was in danger, Augustine asserted it could not, for "suicide
is an act which precluded the possibility of repentance, and
it is a form of homicide and thus a violation of the Decalogue
Article, 'Thou shalt not kill.' "

The earliest organizational disapproval of suicide was
expressed by the Second Council of Orleans in 533.
Churches were permitted to receive offerings on behalf of
those who were killed in the commission of a crime provided
they did not lay violent hands on themselves. Suicide was
regarded as the most serious and heinous of all transgres-
sions. In 563 the Fifteenth Canon of the Council of Braga
denied the suicide the funeral rites of the Eucharist and the

singing of psalms. The Council of Hereford in 673 withheld burial rites to those who died through self-destruction. In 1284, the Synod of Nîmes refused suicides even quiet interment in holy ground.

A further and perhaps more refined elaboration of the Augustinian concept was given by Thomas Aquinas (1224–74). Aquinas opposed suicide on the basis of three postulates: (1) it was against the natural inclinations of preservation of life and charity toward the self; (2) suicide was a trespass against the community; and (3) it was a trespass against God, who had given humankind life. For Saint Thomas, all life was a preparation for the eternal. His argument stressed the sacredness of human life and absolute submission to God.

The philosophical currents of the seventeenth century brought new views of suicide. At that period of history, religious authority was being questioned and undermined. John Donne, (1572–1631), the dean of Saint Paul's Cathedral and well-known poet, was to start a reaction against the existing attitudes of the church toward suicide. When he was a youth, he himself had contemplated taking his life. In his book *Biathanatos* he made a plea for charity and understanding. He viewed suicide neither as a violation of the law nor as contrary to reason. His position was echoed by many secular writers and philosophers. Hume, Montesquieu, Voltaire, and Rousseau wrote essays defending suicide under certain conditions, and argued for the greater freedom of the individual against ecclesiastical authorities.

In modern times, Dietrich Bonhoeffer viewed suicide as a sin in that it represented a denial of God. "God has reserved to Himself the right to determine the end of life, because He alone knows the goal to which it is His will to lead it." Yet Bonhoeffer suspended this judgment for prisoners of war, who might take their own lives rather than reveal information that would injure and destroy the lives of others. The issues of motivation and the greater good were the significant qualifications. Other theologians were less strict about considering suicide as a sin under *all* circumstances.

Not all Christian groups are bound to a rigid code of ethics. The situational, or contextual, ethics of Anglican theologians like Joseph Fletcher and John Robinson represent a change from the attitude of absolute condemnation. They argue that the question of suicide is an open one that must take into account the particular situation, the uniqueness of each human relationship, and the distinctiveness of each person. As Bishop Robinson suggests: "Truth finds expression in different ages."

Today, many clergy view the question of suicide not only from the theological level, but also consider the deep psychic causes and also the sociological implications. Ethical-religious approaches are counterbalanced with the broader perspectives of the social sciences. Increasingly, suicide is being recognized not only as a religious question but as a major medical problem.

For this reason, denominations such as the Anglican Church, taking into consideration modern research, appointed commissions to revise the harsh religious laws regarding suicide. The Lutheran Church in America does not regard suicide as an "unforgivable sin," and Lutherans who take their own lives are not denied a Christian burial.

In the Catholic Church, a directive was issued to priests in the archdiocese of Boston relative to Canon 1240 of the Code of Canon Law, which forbids Christian burial to "persons guilty of deliberate suicide." The late Richard Cardinal Cushing interpreted the law in this way:

> The Church forbids Christian burial to suicides, but only if they were in full possession of their faculties at the time of the crime. The element of notoriety must be present in a suicide for the penalty to be incurred. Hence, no matter how culpable it may have been, if it is not publicly known that the act was fully deliberate, if the

culpability is known only to a few discreet people, burial is not to be denied. Ordinarily there is
not too great a difficulty in granting Christian
burial to a suicide, since most people these days
consider the fact of suicide to be a sign of at least
temporary insanity.

For these reasons, former Bishop Thomas J. Riley of Saint
Peter's Catholic Church in Cambridge stated that he could
not recall a single case in Massachusetts of Christian burial
being denied a suicide.

▶ Islam

In Islam, suicide is the gravest sin. By committing suicide
one violates *kismet*. Faithful Muslims await their destiny;
they do not snatch it from the hands of God. Suicide is
expressly forbidden in the Koran.

And yet among some Muslims, heroic or altruistic suicide is encouraged. Acts of self-destruction are performed
on behalf of God and country. One need only view the faces
of young Iranians who use their bodies to detonate enemy
mines in a mood of exultation; their state of mind is far from
that of people who take their lives in desperation and
despair.

▶ Japanese Religious Faiths

Suicide reached its greatest proportions in Japan, where it
was embedded in religious and national tradition. Compulsory suicide was a form of punishment meted out only
to offenders of noble birth. They could expiate their crimes
and "save face" by dying at their own hands rather than
by the sword of the public executioner. Elaborate ceremonies
attended these rites.

Voluntary *hara-kiri* was committed for revenge and for
other reasons: to protest the policies of a feudal chief or to

follow one's lord into the next world. A situation in which honor was involved meant self-destruction without personal choice. The entire population was affected by the practice of the noble samurai, the Japanese warrior caste who distinguished themselves by their fervent patriotism, indomitable courage, and self-abnegation. In World War II, Japanese kamikaze pilots volunteered to fly their munitions-loaded planes into enemy battleships. Heroic suicide is most prevalent in cultures that have strong group ties and loyalties to both country and religion.

► Critique

There are clergy who may consider suicide to be self-murder. Reverence for existence and patience in suffering are powerful and profound ethical attitudes that have ingrained themselves deeply. Georg Wilhem Hegel (1730–1831) reminds us that "it is the essence of the Spirit to suffer death and nevertheless to remain alive." Suicide is an action that denies the value of human life.

But just as jurists have revoked antisuicide statutes, so have religious leaders reconsidered the concept of suicide. What is accomplished by an ignominious funeral or by asserting that suicide is a heinous crime punishable in hell? Dr. Stanley F. Yolles, former director of the National Institute of Mental Health, states: "Anyone wishing to remove suicide from the sphere of ethics to treat suicide clinically becomes involved with *religious-philosophical prejudices* toward suicide and must overcome them if the suicide program is to be effective." Religious-moral-social revulsion against suicide only blocks understanding of what Albert Camus called a "fatal game that leads from lucidity in the face of existence to flight from light."

No one is suggesting that suicide is desirable or commendable. But it must be underscored that a species that has the power to annihilate nature with nuclear weapons should be less self-righteous and more understanding of its own members. Instead of issuing thundering pronouncements, clergy may better serve their fellow humans by delving into the suicidal person's complex physical and psychological makeup, and then sharing the religious resources of love and understanding. Say the sages: "Do not judge your neighbor until you are in his or her place."

3 ▶ Suicide: The Theorists

Misinformation and prejudice permeate the complex subject of suicide. Social scientists have therefore dedicated themselves to a clearer knowledge of its psychopathology in order to aid in the detection and understanding of persons with suicidal tendencies. It must be stated at the outset that there is no complete agreement even among the great theoreticians. Each scholar and discipline sees the question in a somewhat different light.

▶ Sigmund Freud (1856–1939)

The "founder of psychoanalysis" authored the earliest psychological explanation of suicide. On 27 April 1910, the Vienna Psychoanalytic Society held a discussion on "Suicide in Children." Freud stated that in their zeal to wean children from their early family life, the schools often exposed the immature student too abruptly to the severities of adult life. He said that too little was known about suicide but that perhaps the act was really a repudiation of life because of the craving for death. This remark foreshadowed Freud's later belief in a death instinct.

26

His essay *Mourning and Melancholia* presents his theory of suicide. There are two kinds of drives: one is the life instinct, or *Eros*; the other is the drive toward death, destruction, and aggression, or *Thanatos*. For Freud, death is more than a bodily event. Death is willed. There is a constant shifting of the balance of power of the two polar instincts. Eros ages; ageless Thanatos may assert itself "until it, at length, succeeds in doing the individual to death."

Suicide and murder are aspects of the impulsive and devastating action of Thanatos. Murder is aggression turned upon another; suicide is aggression turned upon the self. Freud's implicit value judgment is that murder is to be disapproved and prevented. Suicide, too, is murder turned about, and must also be disapproved and prevented.

▶ Karl Menninger (b. 1893)

Menninger agrees with Freud that there is a tension in life between the instinct toward self-preservation and the instinct toward self-destructiveness. His own close scrutiny of the deeper motives for suicide posits three elements.

First, there is the *wish to kill*. This element is reflected in the rage of infants when their desires are frustrated. "Just as suckling children resent weaning and feel that something is taken away from them that is their right to possess, so these people who are predominantly infantile cannot stand thwarting." The wish to kill is turned back upon the "wisher" and translated into action as suicide.

Another element is the *wish to be killed*. Just as killing is the extreme form of aggression, so being killed is the extreme form of submission. The demands of conscience are so relentless that there is no inner peace. In order to be punished, people often put themselves in circumstances in which they must suffer. They need to atone by being destroyed.

A final element is the *wish to die*. This is illustrated in the impulses of daredevil drivers or mountain climbers who need to expose themselves to constant danger. The wish to die is extremely widespread, too, among the mentally ill—patients who believe that the only release from their mental anguish is death.

▶ Alfred Adler (1870–1937)

"To be a human being means to feel inferior." This is fundamental to Alfred Adler's "individual psychology." The inability to solve life's problems motivates individuals to strive to overcome their inferiority. But when some persons fail, they need to destroy those around them. Suicide thus signifies a veiled attack upon others. Through an act of self-destruction, they hope to evoke sympathy for themselves and cast reproach upon those responsible for their lack of self-esteem. Adler described suicidal persons as inferiority-ridden people who "hurt others by dreaming themselves into injuries or by administering them to themselves."

▶ Carl Jung (1875–1961)

Jung stressed the unconscious longing for spiritual rebirth as an essential element of self-imposed death. People not only seek to escape intolerable conditions in the present by killing themselves, they also hasten their metaphorical return to their mother's womb. They would then become the safe and secure reborn infant. The picture language of the symbolized wisdom of the ages ("archetype") contains the celebrated Crucifixion: death brings a reward of new life through resurrection.

▶ James Hillman

Perhaps the most forceful defender of the decision to commit suicide is the Jungian analyst James Hillman. He views the preventive approaches of law, medicine, and theology as major stumbling blocks to an adequate understanding of suicide.

For too long, says Hillman, the view of suicide has been colored by moralistic attitudes and the irrational idea that it must be prevented at all costs. Medicine has never honestly come to grips with the problem since physicians are dedicated to prolonging life. The legal tradition has said, in effect: We might kill others in many ways and on many grounds without breaking the law; but, hypocritically, we can never under any circumstances justifiably or excusably kill ourselves. And the clergy oppose suicide not because the act contradicts God but by "reason of fallacious theological dogma."

Hillman believes that suicide is a meaningful and legitimate way of entering death which can "release the most profound fantasies of the human soul." He quotes metaphysician David Hume: "When I fall upon my sword therefore I receive my death equally from the hands of the Deity as if it has proceeded from a lion, a precipice, or a fever."

► Harry Stack Sullivan (1892–1949)

Sullivan postulated an interpersonal theory of psychology. Just as electrons are moved by magnetic attractions, so individuals respond to other persons who are significant to them. The crucial point is the individual's relationships with other people. Every individual has three personifications of "me." When a person feels secure, he or she is the "good me"; in a state of anxiety, a person becomes the "bad me"; in psychotic nightmares, one becomes the "not me." The person evaluates him- or herself in terms of the reaction of significant others toward him/her.

When security is threatened and the crisis is unresolved, conflicts and anxieties become unbearable. The suicidal person may wish to transform the "bad me" into the "not me." Self-destruction is an attractive alternative for the depressed, self-deprecating individual. Suicide represents a hostile attitude toward other people—the outer world—redirected against the self.

▶ Karen Horney (1885–1952)

Although first trained as a Freudian analyst in Germany, Horney later broke with the classical psychoanalytic movement and rejected Freud's instinct theory. If infants were given an anxiety-free environment, she said, they would grow and prosper. However, culture, religion, politics, and other similar forces conspire to distort the child's self-development.

Insecure children think of the world as a hostile place to live. This causes a basic anxiety. Suicide results from childish dependency and from deep-rooted feelings of inferiority, or what Horney calls the "idealized image" one has of him- or herself. It may be a "performance suicide," springing from a sense of failure in meeting the standards expected by society. To Horney, suicide results from a combination of personality characteristics and environment.

▶ Emile Durkheim (1858–1917)

Horney was not the first to speak about the importance of the social context. The landmark of sociological research is Emile Durkheim's pioneering effort of 1897, *Le Suicide*. Durkheim asserted that suicide, which was then considered a highly individual phenomenon, was more explicable as a reaction to the peculiarities of society. The incidence of self-destruction could be accurately traced to the social conditions of the person attempting it. Durkheim was successful in tying suicide—the act of one individual—to the environment in which she or he lives.

It was Durkheim's theory that there are three types of suicide. Most suicides are *egoistic*. Self-destruction occurs because the individual feels alienated and disconnected from community, family, and friends. There is also *anomic* (from *anomie*, meaning "lawlessness") suicide, which represents the failure of the person to adjust to social change. Such suicides occur in times of business crisis, such as an economic depression, or in an era of prosperity, when suicide may be committed by the *nouveaux riches* who are unable to adjust to new standards of living. Last is the *altruistic* suicide, in which the group's authority over the individual is so compelling that the individual loses his or her own personal identity and wishes to sacrifice a life for the community.

▶ Norman L. Faberow

Dr. Faberow is a research psychologist who has worked primarily in the field of suicide prevention for more than a quarter of a century. A former president of the International Association for Suicide Prevention, he helped initiate a worldwide movement that resulted in the establishment of more than 200 suicide prevention centers in the United States alone.

In his book *The Many Faces of Suicide* (1980) Faberow was the first to define and systematically examine those forms of self-destructive behavior which are not generally classified as suicidal, such as substance abuse, including drugs, alcohol, and tobacco; physical illness such as cardiac conditions and spinal injuries where patients disregard their prescribed medical regimen; crime, prostitution, delinquency, compulsive gambling, and other social behavior that carries a greater potential for personal disaster; and high-risk sports such as skydiving, hang gliding, and scuba diving. Faberow adds: "Society values stress-seeking behavior in terms of its lending excitement to life, increasing intensity of feeling, and stimulating exploration of the unknown and expansion of the new."

▶ Edwin S. Schneidman

Dr. Schneidman was the first director of the Center for Studies of Suicide Prevention. In 1957 he collaborated with Norman Faberow in *Clues to Suicide*. Four years later they wrote *The Cry for Help*. Both are classics in the field of suicidology.

In his provocative 1980 volume *Deaths of a Man*, Schneidman catalogues from his many clinical observations those classes of individuals who play a direct and often conscious role in bringing about their own death. *Death-seekers* take their lives intentionally in such a manner that rescue is impossible or unlikely. *Death-initiators* include those terminally ill patients who remove their life-supporting tubes and needles. *Death-darers* are those who, in gambling parlance, bet their lives on a relatively low probability that they will survive, as in Russian roulette, in which the chances of survival are only five out of six. Then there are the *death-welcomers* who, although they play no active role in expediting their death, can honestly state that they would desire an end of life. This is common among troubled youths and the abandoned elderly. In short, "death is hastened by the individual's carelessness, imprudence, foolhardiness, forgetfulness or some other psychological mechanism."

▶ A. Alvarez

Often there is a lack of empathy on the part of therapists treating suicidal patients, A. Alvarez has remarked. This is manifested by the counselors' verbal and facial expressions of anger, premature discharge of the patient, and reduction of the frequency of psychotherapeutic sessions. The reasons for this reaction may be because the suicide of a patient would be a reflection of the therapist's incompetency or the counselor's inability to come to terms with suicidal impulses in him- or herself.

The Savage God (1971) is Alvarez's intense, compassionate, and profound exploration of suicide. "I have to admit that I am a failed suicide. . . . On Friday night I had a terrible dream. I was dancing a savage, stamping dance with my wife full of anger and mutual threat . . . I assume now that when death finally comes, it will probably be nastier than suicide and certainly a great deal less convenient." He concluded by quoting Henry James: "Life is, in fact, a battle. Evil is insolent and strong; beauty enchanting but rare."

▶ Elisabeth Kübler-Ross

No overview of theorists would be complete without the name of Elisabeth Kübler-Ross. She practiced general medicine in Switzerland before coming to the United States, and began her work in death studies while teaching psychiatry at the University of Chicago. Her landmark bestseller *On Death and Dying* (1969), as well as her workshops, lectures, and seminars have made her the most prominent spokesperson in the field of bereavement and grief.

Dr. Ross is famous for examining the various stages that one may experience when facing death. *Denial:* "It wouldn't happen to me—a mistake. You must be talking about someone else." Disbelief acts as a buffer after the unexpected shocking news. *Anger:* this can be released in any direction. The brunt of a person's fury may be directed at a group as well as an individual. Forms of hostility include rage, envy, and resentment. The medical staff of a hospital are frequently the objects of this anger: "Doctors are no good. The only thing they care about is their golf game. They are performing the wrong tests. Incorrect medication is being administered." *Bargaining:* this takes the form of bargaining for one's life: "If I promise to stay away from the race track, will you let me live?" "If you make me well, I promise never to cheat on my wife again." "Let's cut the cards. High card I live and low card I die." *Depression:* this can be a form of anticipatory grief. Everything looks grim. We feel naked, unprotected. We are the prophets of our own doom. We are often noncommunicative at this time because we have lost interest in life. *Acceptance:* during this stage the individual will be able to mourn the impending loss and contemplate death with some degree of quiet expectation. Some writers, such as Abraham Maslow, use the term "self-actualization." "I have led a complete and full life. Therefore, I look forward to death." It may be noted that many psychiatrists believe that less than 2 percent of the population ever experiences this stage.

Dr. Ross addresses the subject of suicide by listing the categories of those seriously ill patients who contemplate taking their lives: (1) those who have a strong need to be in control of everybody and everything; (2) those who are told harshly that they have an incurable disease and "there is nothing else we can do for you because you came for help too late"; (3) potential organ-transplant patients who are given an unrealistic assessment about receiving the life-saving organ; (4) and finally, those patients who are ignored and isolated by friends and family and receive inadequate medical help in their crisis. Some may not take their lives directly. Instead "they break the rules by not taking their medication. In that manner, the patients semipassively promote their own death."

Some of the most prominent social scientists are mentioned in this chapter. Yet no single theory of suicide is definitive. Each individual has his or her own combination of reasons.

4 ▶ *Suicide:*
The Social Context

Emile Durkheim demonstrated how environmental factors such as economic conditions, marital status, race, and religion are related to the pressures of a life situation. Suicide reflects an individual's view not only of him- or herself, but of a relationship to the community as well. Knowledge of the various sociological factors associated with suicide may be helpful in evaluating the risks for the individual.

▶ Economic Conditions

It has often been said that suicide is the luxury of the wealthy. This is simply not true. For all classes, economic distress brings a sense of hopelessness and despair. Suicides are found in blighted areas in ghettos and locations where retired people attempt to subsist on insufficient pensions and welfare programs.

For the very poor as well as for the rich, the rate of suicide soars during periods of economic depression. However, those with the highest-status positions react more violently to fluctuations in business. During the Depression of 1930–43, the greatest increase in suicide occurred among the more prosperous. Wealth, the highest token of success, had been lost. The sense of well-being among the wealthy rests on a bedrock of buying power. When that is gone, their sense of competence and identity are challenged and called into question.

The less wealthy suffer as well. There has been a marked increase of suicide among farmers in the United States. With the loss of their farms, there ensues a weakened family structure as the household is forced to create a whole new way of life. When the employment level is high and the country prospers, the suicide rate is lower. Economic recessions, business reverses, and the loss of employment— all have powerful psychological consequences.

▶ Occupation

A person's job or profession is clearly a factor in suicide. University of Oregon researchers studied self-inflicted deaths in that state for a period of eleven years. They found that suicides among doctors, dentists, and lawyers were three times as common as among nonprofessional white-collar workers.

The suicide rate among physicians in the United States is 28 to 40 per 100,000, compared to 12.3 per 100,000 among the general population. Doctors run at least twice the risk as the rest of the country. A 1987 study in the *Journal of the American Medical Association* discovered that female physicians are four times more likely than other women to commit suicide, although their rate is about the same as that of male doctors. Dr. Douglas A. Sargent reflected: "Physicians are good at taking care of other people but often not very good at taking care of ourselves or each other." Dr. Werner Simon states that the medical specialists at highest risk are anesthesiologists, ophthalmologists, and especially psychiatrists.

According to the American Psychiatric Association, the annual suicide rate for psychiatrists is 70 per 100,000 or four times as great as that for the general population. One-third of the psychiatrists who took their lives did so during the earlier years of their professional practice. A 1986 joint study by the American Medical Association and American Psychiatric Association of 142 physicians who killed themselves discovered that many had abused drugs or alcohol or had suffered professional, personal, and/or financial losses.

Positions of leadership and responsibility can cause unbearable anxieties, especially for managers of large corporations. Rapid technological advances may make their skills outmoded. When mergers of large companies occur, executives may discover that their once secure position has been eliminated. In desperation they may react with somatic disturbances, family discord, alcoholism, and, finally, suicide.

► Male and Female

Although the female suicide rate has been increasing, male suicides still outnumber those of females. "It is clear that at present, there is no support for statements that sex differences are declining in the United States and that soon females will kill themselves as frequently or more frequently, than males" (John McIntosh, *Suicide and Life-Threatening Behavior*, Spring 1986). Currently, men kill themselves at a rate of nearly 4 to 1 over women. For men 65 to 85 years old, the ratios increase with age from 4 to 6 to 9 male suicides for every suicide by a female.

And yet three-quarters of those who attempt suicide are women, most often between the ages of fifteen and forty. On the other hand, three-quarters of completed suicides are male. One explanation for this is in the method of suicide: women are generally more concerned about what happens to their bodies after death. Historically, most men have committed suicide by hanging, shooting, or jumping from heights. The majority of women almost always use passive means of self-destruction, i.e., sleeping pills, poison, or gas. Swallowing barbiturates is less disfiguring than a gunshot wound to the head. Many experts believe that as women learn more about the lethal potential of certain drugs, and begin to show a greater willingness to use more violent means such as hanging and shooting, that the suicide rate among women will escalate.

One may ask: Is there a difference of motive between the suicidal man and woman? Dr. Marv Miller, a consultant in suicidology, observes:

> Female suicides seem to occur in reaction to romantic or marital problems which tend to appear and be resolved fairly early in life. Male suicides are more likely to be a reaction to extreme physical problems or what has been termed 'downward mobility'—the loss of employment, income, and status. These problems usually arrive later in life, often coincide with the onset of retirement, and are not so easily resolved. While female suicides are primarily a phenomenon of youth and young adulthood, the male suicide rate increases with each succeeding decade of age.

▶ Marital Status

Students of epidemiology have consistently reported that suicide is less frequent among married persons. However, there is one noticeable exception: the young married population. The rate of suicide for those under the age of twenty-four is much higher for married than for single persons. This reversal is most dramatic for those under the age of twenty—teen-agers who may have rushed into an ill-advised marriage to escape an unsatisfactory home environment or who have been forced into a wedding because of pregnancy. After age twenty-four, the odds favor the married individual. As Durkheim reported as early as the nineteenth century, early marriage has an "aggravating influence on suicide."

The suicide rate until the age of thirty-five is higher for the widowed than for the single person. Problems facing the young widow or widower are especially severe. The death of the husband or wife often comes at a time when the couple was actively engaged in raising a family and paying the mortgage on their home. Death shatters not only the emotional life of the survivor but abruptly leaves him or her to cope with difficult family responsibilities alone. Widowed individuals are at the greatest risk during the first year of the death of a spouse.

After the age of thirty-five, the suicide rate of the single person is higher than that of those who have experienced the death of a spouse. Children play an important part in helping the widowed person feel needed. The young give meaning to the parent's existence. In contrast, the single person may feel adrift without a caring family. The future suggests only more alienation and social desolation.

The suicide rate for divorced persons is four to five times that for married persons. Divorce is a kind of death. Divorce may mean not only the loss of a companion, a helper around the house, cook and laundress, carpenter and plumber, father-figure or mother figure. There can also be the loss of a home, the custody of children, and friends. Separation means no longer being part of a "we" relationship. Now it is "I." Divorce means saying "goodbye" to hopes, promises, and dreams.

In summary, people who are at the greatest risk for suicide are those who have never been married, followed by those who are widowed, separated, or divorced; those who are married and have no child; and finally, those who are married and have children.

▶ Youth

Young people are killing themselves in epidemic numbers. Every day over 1,000 youths attempt to destroy themselves.

For every teenager who succeeds, another 100 will try and fail.

Suicide among adolescents has almost tripled in the last decade. It is the second leading cause of death in young people today. While the highest incidence is for young people between the ages of 15 and 24, new startling statistics indicate that suicide among youngsters aged 5 to 14 has increased eightfold in the last 30 years. In addition, experts even believe that many so-called "accidental" deaths involving automobiles, drugs, and firearms are actually disguised suicides.

While teen-age suicide is a frightening subject, it can no longer be avoided or evaded. Contrary to common belief, discussing suicide will not place ideas into young people's heads that were not already there or lead them to self-execution. In fact, a recent national survey revealed over 70 percent of teens felt suicide could best be prevented through suicide awareness programs for youth and their parents.

"She had every reason to live. Why would she do it?" While there is no single reason why a teenager will take his or her own life, a leading factor of adolescent suicide is a pervading sense of hopelessness and helplessness. Problems at that critical moment appear overpowering with no solutions or changes in sight. One eighteen-year-old having difficulty relating to others said, "I am alone in a tunnel that never ends. It keeps getting darker and darker."

Young people who attempt to commit suicide often have low self-esteem, a sense of worthlessness. A high-school student who was perceived by others as an outstanding athlete felt that he didn't measure up. "I'm okay in sports, but I should be the best." Often, adolescents' expectations or those of their parents are unrealistic. Teenagers may even believe that their families would be better off without them. They feel like biological strangers, that they are out of step and do not fit into the family circle. Or they may have the feeling (often for no reason) of being unwanted, perhaps assuming their birth was not desired, a phenomenon aptly described as "the discarded child."

Experiencing the loss of a relationship is another significant event that may precede the suicide of a young person—a broken romance, moving to a different home, or a family loss through death or divorce. There is an abrupt loss of meaningful supports and attachments. A strong correlation also exists between the onset of self-destructive behavior in adolescents and a family history of cruelty, violence, rejection, or abandonment.

Suicidal youths rarely wish to die; they just wish to escape what they consider to be an intolerable condition. "If I were dead, I wouldn't hurt so much," said a high-school senior who was depressed because he was not admitted to the college of his choice. Unfortunately, those close to the troubled student failed to detect his pain, listen to his feelings, and express their love. He took his life.

Myths about teenage suicide must be dispelled; they could cost a child's life.

▶ *Myth:* "Those who talk about suicide rarely attempt or commit it."

▶ *Fact:* Most of the young people who have attempted or committed suicide have given significant verbal clues as to their intentions.

▶ *Myth:* "The tendency toward suicide is inherited."

▶ *Fact:* There is no evidence of genetic predisposition to suicide. However, young people are especially suggestible, and a previous suicide in the family could establish a destructive model for repeat behavior.

▶ *Myth:* "Nothing could have stopped her once she decided to take her life."

▶ *Fact:* Most adolescents who contemplate suicide are torn

between a desire to live and a desire to die. They want their suffering to end and, at the same time, wish to find an alternative or a solution to their pain. Too often, their cry for help goes unheard by families, friends, and even professionals.

▶ *Myth:* "Suicidal youths are mentally ill."

▶ *Fact:* Most young people who attempt or commit suicide would not be diagnosed as "mentally ill." Of course, chronic mental illness does increase the risk.

▶ *Myth:* "A teenager who experiences a suicidal episode is never out of danger even when he or she becomes an adult."

▶ *Fact:* Many depressed youths are helped and do recover to lead normal, healthy lives. What can help keep them alive is our becoming more aware of the warning signs and of the ways to respond to troubled, potentially suicidal young people.

Much can be done to prevent adolescent suicide. In a survey taken at the University of Southern California it was learned that less than half of the students shared their depressed feelings with parents. Many suicides occurred at home, very often with the parents in the next room. It was reported that in many instances lack of communication between parent and child is a significant factor in the young people's desire to take their lives.

It becomes obvious that a better relationship between adult and child will help reduce the incidence of teenage suicide. Breakdowns frequently occur when parents substitute their authority for honest responses to their children's concerns. Adults could spend more undistracted time listening to their adolescents and trying to comprehend what they are really saying and thinking. Young people also have a responsibility to understand adult views and values. Children and parents need not agree on all issues in order to communicate more effectively with each other. They can demonstrate in word and in touch that even though there are differences, there is still unconditional love and support.

▶ Middle Age

Middle age is often considered to be the state of attainment. As such, these years have come to represent that time in life when no crucial developmental problems arise. It is taken for granted that in the middle years the individual is able to achieve full personhood and mature into complete economic and physical independence.

For these reasons social scientists have directed their research and exploration almost entirely toward the problems and issues of youth and old age. Over the years, however, changes in technology have changed the profile of the population, as well as attitudes and awareness about the middle years. D. J. Levinson's *The Seasons of a Man's Life,* B. L. Neugarten's *The Awareness of Middle Ages,* and S. Osherson's *Grieving for a Lost Self at Midlife* have extended the developmental theory through the *entire* life cycle. Gail Sheehy's *Passages* sold millions of copies, revealing the degree of interest among readers between 35 and 55 years of age who were entering, immersed in, or emerging from a midlife crisis. The conclusion is that there is turmoil in the middle years and a rise in the frequency of suicide.

Depression is the most common psychiatric illness experienced during middle age. Greying hair and deepening lines are sharp reminders of life's relentless forward march. Excess weight, baldness, and worsening eyesight occur between ages 40 and 60. The fear of becoming less able sexually is common to many persons in their middle forties, when men in particular still measure their masculinity by their sexual performance.

Like men, women are often acutely conscious of bodily changes that occur during this time, and they often begin to feel unattractive, unwanted, and useless. Physical illness becomes more common in a middle-aged man with myocardial infarction or a woman with breast cancer. The death of contemporaries provokes the realization that the same thing could just as easily happen to them. Middle-age depression can lead to suicide.

Along with physiological alteration comes psychological change. Parents who once supported their children may now be dependent on them. Very often, menopause begins just as children leave home permanently and husbands become less supportive because they are absorbed in their own concerns. There are also endless marital and familial conflicts with spouse and children that result in behavioral changes. Infidelity and divorce can be yet another source of distress and crisis.

A mood of despondency can invade not only family life but a career as well. An individual's hopes and goals have not been realized and are in fact now perceived to be unrealizable. A sought-after position is given to a "younger" person because of our society's tremendous emphasis on youth. (Today, a majority of the presidents of large corporations are in their forties.) For others the challenge is no longer there, or there is professional stagnation.

In general terms, the pattern goes like this: A rising young executive, aflame with creative ideas, moves through a series of regular promotions. Then in what should be highly productive middle years, she or he suddenly burns out. Some contemplate midlife career changes to remake their lives; others just despair and go through the motions of existence both at home and in their careers. They think: "What good is it all? All I have ahead of me is more failure and defeat." Lost are the grandiose fantasies and visions of youth. The absence of true self-definition, separation from childhood, and the fear of old age are unsettling and devastating. To those suffering the misery of loss of self at midlife, death appears as a release.

Suicides increase during the middle years. Statistics indicate that in one twelve-month period there were 1,400 suicides of Americans aged 30–34; 1,800 in the 35–39 age bracket; more than 2,000 in the 40–44 and in the 45–49 brackets; and more than 2,200 among Americans aged 50–54.

▶ The Elderly

The poet Robert Browning said in his poem "Rabbi Ben Ezra":

> Grow old along with me!
> The best is yet to be,
> The last of life, for which the first was made.

People await their senior years. Age is supposed to bring peace to troubled souls. Yet the suicide rate for older people is the highest of any age group.

Every year over 10,000 Americans over age 60 will kill themselves. Although those 65 and over comprise only 11 percent of the population, they account for 25 percent of all suicides. Alarming as these statistics may appear, they represent a drastic underreporting of the true incidence. Elderly people may easily disguise their lethal intentions by taking an overdose of drugs, mixing medicines, failing to take life-sustaining medication, or by literally starving themselves to death.

Old age is not the season of vanity. The skin is wrinkled; the body is stooped. It is as if one is being ravaged by an unseen enemy.

Old age brings physical infirmities as well. Nearly nine out of ten elderly people have one or more chronic health problems. Hearing loss is the most widespread impairment associated with aging. Partial deafness causes anxiety, maladjustment, and isolation.

Vision changes with age. Muscles that control pupil dilation for light adaptation are altered. There is a higher incidence of glaucoma (increased pressure) and cataracts (clouding of the lens). Visual loss curtails or eliminates pastimes such as reading, watching television, doing handwork, and joining in social activities.

In addition, the aging process involves modifications in the nervous system, in muscle tone, reflex action, posture control, balance, and equilibrium. Thermal senses can be impaired. The sex drive is diminished. There are memory problems because of arteriosclerosis, side effects of medication, depression, and anxiety.

There are personal losses as well. Death robs the elderly of siblings, their spouses, colleagues, friends, even their adult children. Without employment, the compensations of work disappear—not just the necessity of money but also the self-esteem and satisfactions that provided the structure of their earlier years.

In the aging process one loss leads to another: decline of physical health, decreased activity, lowered earning capacity, loss of independence, changes in relationships with family and friends, physical and social isolation, mental illness, and depression. Old age can indeed be a losing game. No wonder that older Americans are deadly serious about killing themselves.

Certain groups among the aged are more at risk. Among whites, men over the age of 65 have suicide rates four times the national average, and the rate for women in this age group is two times the average. White men are ten times as likely to commit suicide as women. Overall among the elderly suicide rates are lower among nonwhites than among whites.

Earlier studies of suicide reported a higher prevalence among upper socioeconomic classes of older people, but today most researchers indicate high rates among those in the lower economic classes as well. Elderly urban dwellers are at the highest risk, especially those in inner-city developments.

Many physicians and social scientists seem unaware of the seriousness of the problem of suicide among the aged. A number of studies have shown that most elderly persons who kill themselves consult a physician shortly before the suicide. It is reported that 76 percent of older men who took their lives had seen a doctor within one month before their suicides, 33 percent had gone within one week, and as many as 10 percent of aged persons who kill themselves had gone to a physician on that very day or just before the event. The doctors were not able to discern that their somatic complaints—behavioral and verbal indicators—were signaling an intent to self-destruction. Alcoholism and drug abuse among the elderly are also not often recognized.

In the United States today there are as many persons over the age of 65 as there are adolescents. By the year 2025, there will be twice as many older persons as teenagers. More than 5,000,000 Americans reach the age of 65 every year. In the year 1900, there were approximately 3 million persons over the age of 65 in our country. We now have over 26 million.

Society has the responsibility to be more concerned about the status roles, economic and emotional security, and the social isolation of older people. Successive White House conferences on aging have elicited the obvious goals of the aged: (1) increase in social security and pension benefits; (2) better preparation for retirement and abolition of compulsory retirement age; (3) provision of more and safer housing for the elderly; (4) improved public transportation; and (5) better nutrition and health care delivery. Unfortunately, little action has been taken. If the general population has no meaningful answers to their questions—"I'm not worth anything to anyone anymore. What good am I? Why doesn't God take me already?"—the suicide rate for older Americans will continue to increase.

▶ Cities and Neighborhoods

Isolation, whether geographical, social, or emotional, is an important factor in suicide. With increasing urbanization and mobility, families, friends, and communities are less closely knit, and the organizations and roles that have given meaning to a person's life are painfully removed. Hence suicide rates increase when people leave behind their roots for a life that has fewer social networks.

Downward social mobility resulting from job loss or retirement has a direct relationship to suicide. When the elderly are moved to unfamiliar surroundings with fewer interpersonal relationships, feelings of hopelessness and uselessness ensue. Three Florida cities with a disproportionately high number of aged and infirm people have an inordinately high suicide rate. As compiled by the National Center for Health Statistics for the 50 largest metropolitan areas in the United States, the highest rate in the nation is that of Tampa–St. Petersburg, at 18.9 per 100,000, followed by Fort Lauderdale–Hollywood at 18.18; Miami's rate is 16.0.

The suicide curve climbs as one moves west and then becomes greatest in the mountain and Pacific states. The rate in the Denver–Boulder area is third in the nation, at 18.0, followed by San Francisco–Oakland at 16.4. The rate for Phoenix is 15.8, as is that for Sacramento; the rate of California Riverside–San Bernardino–Ontario is 15.3, and San Diego's is 15.0. Hopes are not always achieved in glamorous cities. For those whose dreams are never realized, self-inflicted death can be a last resort.

The suicide rate falls steadily from a high point in cities with a population over 100,000 to a low point in rural areas. This can be attributed to the complex psychological aggravations of city life. Many southern cities such as Chattanooga and Knoxville, Tennessee; Corpus Christi, Texas; and Greensboro, North Carolina boast low suicide rates. In contrast, elderly urban dwellers are at highest risk in inner city environments.

▶ Race

Suicide rates are generally highest for Caucasians. In 1965, Schneidman and Faberow's study revealed that 95 percent of suicides occurred among whites. Later investigations have revealed that suicide among blacks is on the rise, especially among the young. An examination of data compiled by the New York City Bureau of Vital Statistics revealed the surprising information that, among blacks of both sexes between the ages of 20 and 35, suicide was more of a problem than it was among the white population of the same age. After the age of 35, the rate of suicide among blacks levels off. Having survived the concrete jungle, the black male is not as tempted to die in it.

Suicide for black females has risen more than 80 percent in the last twenty years. Dr. Herbert Hendlin described in his pioneering book *Black Suicide* the predicament of the poverty-stricken black woman:

> The most disastrous impact of racial institutions seems to be felt so early in life and so over- whelmingly that the plight seems as bad as that of the male. While the male is harder hit by so- cio-economic pressures, it is often the female who bears the brunt of his anger. Unfortunately, for the most part, black women have been ig- nored in the literature on suicide.

Environments in which there is constant crime and vio- lence, drug abuse, and/or a missing father figure would make anyone more vulnerable to suicide, white or black. Because blacks have the highest unemployment rate with the attendant frustration, rage, and failed social relation- ships, the result is a negative self-image, low self-esteem, feelings of isolation and rejection, and self-destruction.

When blacks migrate to northern industrial centers, their rate of suicide rises markedly. The difficulty experienced in integrating themselves into a different society, a step for which they are not always adequately equipped, leads to *egoistic* self-destruction. They also become more prone to *anomic* suicide because of the higher self-expectations and problems in economic adjustment attendant upon a closer relationship with the white community.

Research tended to focus primarily on members of the white and black races until Dr. Harry L. Dizmany investigated the Native American. He discovered a virtual suicide epidemic among Native Americans between the ages of 15 and 20.

"The Indian adolescent," Dr. Dizmany stated,

> not only experiences a constant struggle to derive
> an individual identity from a highly disrupted
> family setting, but also faces the problem of ac-
> quiring a social identity from a disorganized cul-
> ture. He is caught, in fact, between two cultures:
> one for which he is unprepared, the other which
> he feels has failed him and toward which he has
> a deep ambivalence. He is neither an Indian,
> with a sense of pride and respect for his people
> and his culture, nor an assimilated outsider able
> to identify with the culture and traditions of the
> dominant group. In his adolescence, the Indian
> youth thus begins to experience a diffusion of
> identity and the psychological chaos of not
> knowing who he really is or even why he has
> the right to exist. Suicide then often becomes,
> paradoxically, the only way the Indian male can
> have any sense of control over his destiny.

Certain patterns for suicidal behavior among Native Americans have been documented. Like women in the general population, Native American women are less likely to make suicide attempts than are men. For Native Americans, suicides usually peak in the twenties or early thirties and constantly decline after that point. (In contrast, the peak usually occurs among the elderly in the non-Native population.)

While the suicide rate for Native Americans is greater than that for the rest of the nation, it must be emphasized that there is a wide variance among individual tribes. For example, the Apache suicide rate is extremely high, while there are fewer acts of self-destruction among the Navajo. Because there are such large differences among tribal groups, and often among groups within a single tribe in different geographical locations, we cannot accurately pinpoint the suicide rate among Native Americans as a whole.

Asian Americans also have high suicide rates. The poorest and least acculturated cluster in the inner city, where they suffer from stresses of displacement into a strange culture, interpersonal conflicts, and economic worries that could lead to suicidal impulses, especially among the young. Many children from Southeast Asia who have been adopted by American families are not always able to bridge the gap between values taught in their native land and those of their new environment.

Suicide statistics for minority groups are not accurate. As the Samaritans of Boston discovered when reviewing death certificates, many Asian Americans as well as Hispanics were reported as whites. "Racial" accuracy is often difficult to determine.

Although exact numbers are not known, it is evident that the number of suicides among Hispanics is increasing. Why? The Hispanics' highly developed extended family is often disturbed when they leave a familiar environment for a new land. There is also the obvious difference in language: most prefer to speak Spanish in the home while using English at school and at work. Those who are economically disadvantaged (as opposed to culturally disadvantaged) are concerned with survival on a day-to-day basis. Those who were educated and skilled in their homeland have now lost not only most of their wealth but their influence as well.

Many aliens are uninformed or suspicious of the natural-ization process. And at this writing, there are political exiles who have fled from tyrannical, noncommunist countries who are not recognized by our government as legitimate refugees. Some would rather kill themselves than return to their country of origin and what they consider to be intol-erable conditions or certain death.

▶ Geography

One striking feature of statistics on suicide is the wide dis-parity between countries. At present the highest suicide rate in the world is in West Berlin. Some experts believe that this is because West Berlin is estranged geographically, po-litically, and culturally from its neighbors. A wall divides families from their relatives in East Berlin. Brothers and sis-ters are so close and yet so far.

The other ten nations outside of the Soviet bloc in which the suicide problem has been the greatest during the twen-tieth century are, in order, Austria, Switzerland, Germany, Denmark, Japan, France, Sweden, Belgium, Luxembourg, and the United States.

Until recently, we knew very little about the suicide rate in Eastern Europe. The Soviet Union did not publish such statistics because suicide "is a bourgeois solution to life's problems." With the advent of *glasnost,* startling revelations have come to light. We now know that countries in the communist bloc have high suicide rates, with Hungary at the top of the list. Yugoslavia has an overall rate of 14.9 per 100,000, and in some provinces it is as great as 30.4—almost two and a half times that of the United States. Suicide does not distinguish between capitalism and communism.

Most of the nations that have a high suicide rate are industrialized and urbanized. The United States, for ex-ample, has an average of 124 persons per 100,000 who take their own lives. In Ireland the figure is 2.7. The lowest rate is found in Egypt (0.3 per 100,000 of the population).

It is difficult to isolate the variables that determine the prevalence of suicide in one country and its absence nearby. The late president Eisenhower once associated suicide with the welfare states of Sweden (18 per 100,000) and Denmark (19 per 100,000). But Norway is also a highly socialized land, and has a lower rate (8.4 per 100,000) than the United States. Also, the high rates in Denmark go back a century or more, predating the welfare state. If anything, the current rate shows a modest decline.

Japan is no longer the most suicidal nation in the world. When that country is mentioned, many immediately think of *shinju*, the love pact suicide, and *hara-kiri*, which means "belly cutting." But mandatory *hara-kiri* has been outlawed for almost a hundred years. However, suicide is especially high among the Japanese youth today. There are tremendous pressures to succeed both in school and the workplace. The precipitating cause may be failing a crucial examination or the inability to attend the college of choice. Failure and the fear of failure have a shattering effect on the sense of competency, self-worth, and the desire to live.

Yet it is impossible to ascertain the frequency of suicide by geographical regions alone, even though many scholars have tried to isolate the contributing factors. Herbert Hendin in his *Suicide in Scandinavia* approached the underlying dynamics by examining child-rearing practices. W. McDougall dealt with England and France by examining the personality predispositions of the Nordic and Mediterranean population. However, it is impossible to isolate the diverse components in each country. There are multitudes of overlapping subcultures with diffuse economic circumstances, customs, and traditions.

► War and Peace

In order to evaluate a nation's suicide rate, one must first define the internal conditions that exist at a particular time. For instance, it has long been known that there is a significant drop in suicides among citizens of all ages during a national war.

A study of prewar, wartime, and postwar suicide rates in ten countries indicates that, in every case, self-imposed death was less frequent from 1915 to 1918 and more frequent again from 1926 to 1930. War is usually a time of patriotism, social integration, and national purpose. Each citizen—male or female, white, black, or yellow, old or young—is needed for the great effort of victory. It is a time of hope not only for military success but for a better world for all humankind. With an increase in purpose, there is a decrease in suicide, especially among males.

Also, through war, people find an honorable way to vent their aggressions, and for this they are rewarded with medals and accolades. In Freud's words: "The willingness to fight may depend upon a variety of motives which may be lofty, frankly outspoken, or unmentionable. The pleasure in aggression and destruction is certainly one of these. The death instinct would destroy the individual were it not turned upon objects rather than the self, so that the individual saves his own life by destroying something external to it." In time of war, there is a greater opportunity for devoting one's energies to externalized aggression, a common enemy.

What happens when war is not sanctioned and members of the armed services return home? Attention is now being directed to those who returned from the unpopular war in Southeast Asia. According to the California Medical Center in San Francisco, Vietnam War veterans are much more likely to die from suicide than those persons of equivalent age who did not enter the armed services. The ordeal or battle does not always end with the cessation of hostilities.

▶ Time of Year

More suicides occur in spring, when one's desolate feelings are confronted by the bloom and burgeoning of nature. The bleakness of winter seems to match one's unhappiness, but there is a glaring contrast between the bright days of spring and the dark self. Historically, spring neuroses are identified with the old seed-sowing festivals and the provocative accompaniment of revelry and celebration. The sharp dichotomy between the smiling spring world and a despairing state of mind is one of the factors in provoking self-imposed death. As the poet T. S. Eliot wrote, "April is the cruelest month." The April suicide rate is the highest for any month and is some 120 percent above the average for the rest of the year.

During the Christmas period there is also a high rate of suicide. Depressed by broken homes, death, loneliness, business and social failures, people find that they are not feeling the joy they expect during the "happy season." Sorrowfully, they resort to taking their own life. A study by the Arthur P. Noyes Institute for Neuro-Psychiatric Research reveals that in December, New Hampshire had its highest number of suicides and also a sharp rise in admissions to mental hospitals.

Some consider the act of suicide a quest for rebirth. *Pastoral Psychology* devoted an entire issue to "Christmas and Suicide." A psychiatrist analyzed how some of his patients identified themselves with the baby Jesus and how the Savior died that the faithful might live. Christmas is part of a "holiday" syndrome, which is distinguished by a desire for a new birth, like that of Jesus, and a magical resolution of the unsettled problems of life.

Dr. Norman Rosenthal, chief of the Unit of Outpatient Studies at the National Institute of Mental Health, has coined a new term, SAD (*Seasonal Affective Disorder*), for those who suffer from holiday "blues" and winter melancholy. When days are short and nights are long and the weather is cold, there is an increase in hospitalization for depressed patients and a rise in suicides.

▶ Media and Cluster Suicides

The evidence increasingly suggests that imitative behavior may play a role in suicide, especially among teenagers. Dr. David Phillips and Lindie L. Carstensen in the *New England Journal of Medicine* (September 1986) described their study of nationally televised news or feature stories and the fluctuation of the suicide rate before and after these events. They concluded that the more networks that carried the story about suicide, the greater was the increase in suicide.

The idea of cluster suicide did not originate with the death of Marilyn Monroe. In 1774, Johann Wolfgang von Goethe published a romantic novel, *The Sorrows of Young Werther*, about an artistically inclined young man, "gifted with deep, pure sentiment, and pentrating intelligence who loses himself in fantastic dreams and undermines himself with speculative thoughts, until finally, torn by hopeless passions, especially by infinite love, he shoots himself in the head." The book was widely read in Europe and was blamed for leading impressionable young people to commit suicide. Authorities not only banned its sale but destroyed copies for fear of a wave of imitative suicides. Hence the term "Werther effect" originated to designate the imitative influence on suicide.

The Werther effect affirms the existence of a statistically significant relationship between media coverage of suicide and an increase in suicide among teenagers. It is also well documented in school: when one youth commits suicide, others may follow. (Clustering seems to be an adolescent phenomenon; in fact, there is no significant peak in suicides among persons 20 years of age and older.)

What prescriptive action can be taken if the evidence suggests that the media's presentation of a suicide may have lethal effects? Dr. Leon Eisenberg of Harvard Medical School states: "We lack the authority, moral or civil to manipulate the media . . . yet, even as we abjure official censorship, we must ask ourselves and our colleagues in the press: 'Why should cases of suicide be recorded at length in the public papers, any more than cases of fever.' " Although the Werther effect is significant enough to warrant further study, it accounts for only a small part of the variation in suicide rates.

▶ Jail Suicides

The incidence of suicide in short-term lockups such as municipal jails is nearly five times that of the general population and nearly six times that in long-term prisons. Everyone placed in a cell is at a high potential suicide risk.

In most states there are suicide prevention measures such as placing clear plastic material over the bars to prevent inmates from tying ropes to them. There are also audio monitoring equipment and a timeclock so that visual cell checks can be made every fifteen minutes. In addition there are screening processes with each suspect's name placed in a computer to determine if the person has a history of suicide attempts.

There are those who feel strongly that it is inadvisable to have plastic coverings over the bars because it can enhance claustrophobic feelings of aloneness. They maintain that it is the isolation and unpleasant environment of the cell that contribute to the high occurrence of lockup suicides. They suggest that, as an alternative suicide prevention measure, someone from personnel (preferably not a uniformed officer) be present within each cell area. (One-on-one observation of this kind is the procedure routinely used in hospitals when a patient is suspected of being a serious suicide risk.) Most important, however, is the improvement of the entire penal system, whereby inmates can be afforded greater dignity, purpose, and rehabilitation.

▶ Homosexuals

A number of large-scale investigations report a significantly high rate of suicide among gay men and lesbians. Three large studies found that gay men and lesbians attempt suicide two to seven times more often than heterosexual comparison groups. Of those who attempt suicide, researchers indicate that 20 to 60 percent will ultimately take their lives. Dr. Herbert Hendin agrees:

> My own experience has led me to think that homosexuals are overrepresented among the most seriously suicidal individuals. . . . What does the young man accomplish in the dream and by the suicide attempt? He gains an illusory control over the situation that involves rejection. In the dream, if there is any rejecting to be done, he is going to do it; by committing suicide, he is the one who leaves or does the rejecting. There is an experience of omnipotence through death.

R. Maris in his article in *Suicide and Life-Threatening Behaviors* attributes the high number of homosexual suicides to their traumatic personal histories in a homophobic society. With the imposition of such alienating factors as economic discrimination and prolonged isolation, "there is little wonder that they have their own special set of social problems including suicide. Society has increasingly disenfranchised them." Social segregation, including reduced or broken ties within personal support networks of lovers, family, and friends, is one of the most reliable correlates of suicide.

Gay men and lesbians are at greater risk of suicide when they are involved with substance abuse. Until recently much of gay men's socializing has centered around gay bars, with few alternatives for meeting in alcohol- and drug-free environments. Substance abuse is also one way to cope with the hatred, isolation, and fear they meet with from their neighbors and family. For the same reason, 75 percent of suicide attempters and 16 percent of suicide completers had been treated for at least one overdose of drugs as well as a history of alcoholism.

It must be emphasized that while gay men and lesbians are at risk for suicide, not *every* homosexual is suicidal. If the national concern about AIDS can be kept from turning into hysteria, if heterosexual bias can be lessened, and if educational programs for suicide prevention and intervention are enacted, the suicide risk could be considerably lowered.

▶ Religion

Since the major religions of this country—Judaism, Catholicism, and Protestantism—disapprove of suicide, one may hypothesize that strongly religious people would not approve of suicide for themselves, their family, or for society. According to Emile Durkheim, religious affiliation is an important factor in determining whether one will die of natural or unnatural causes.

However, other factors are involved besides theology. Dr. Leonardo Magran, chairman of the Albert Einstein Medical Center's Division of Child Development and Child Psychiatry, stated that statistics show suicide is higher among Protestants than among Jews and Catholics. "Jewish families are by and large tighter," he said. "There is more cohesiveness, so suicidal attempts are less common." On the other hand, he noted that "there is a lot of pressure for overachievement in Jewish families." But young people "can withstand the pressures if they have a support system, if not from the family, then from the Jewish community and synagogues."

Dr. Norman Faberow believes that the suicide rate is lower for Jews than the national average because "Jews are too interested in life, production, and creativity for suicide." From the Jewish standpoint, suicide is akin to identifying with the enemy, those who devalued the lives of their martyred ancestors. In addition, there are strong family ties that give them a close relationship to kin and community.

Some researchers believe that Catholics, because they have the strongest taboos against suicide, kill themselves less frequently than members of any other religious faith. The Church brings integration into the adherents' lives with its universal body of common beliefs and dogmas, which includes the belief that suicide is a mortal sin punishable after death. Since Catholics have a strong belief in an afterlife, they would not see suicide as a viable option. Yet, even though belief in punishment after death may deter some Catholics, a desire for reunion with a loved one may be a motive for suicide in other cases.

The highest suicide rate is generally considered to be among the numerous and loosely federated Protestant denominations. However, Catholic and Protestant Ireland both have the same low suicide rate, while Catholic Austria's is the highest of this century.

Experts who have studied the correlation between religion and suicide believe that time, place, and circumstance play an important part no matter what a person's religious background. Today, the ghetto walls have crumbled and the religious and ethnic differences that once separated peoples are gradually disappearing. Religious statistics are difficult to compile. In some states, since death certificates do not indicate religion, compilation of data is woefully incomplete. Even the terms Jew, Protestant, and Catholic are deceiving and deceptive. Is the person a practicing Jew? Does the Catholic attend mass? Is the word Protestant a mark of commitment or a facile title implying "miscellaneous"?

The point is self-evident: on the basis of the statistical study of the relationship between suicide and religious affiliation, simple deductions cannot be effectively tabulated as a single-dimensional technique. Just as different religions may judge suicide differently, so there are variations of attitudes and sociological changes even within the same faith over a period of time. Clearly, the suicide rate is influenced by many factors besides the religion of its population, e.g.,

economic conditions, social traditions, degree of urbanization, and the prevailing political climate. But even more
important than statistics is the most crucial problem of all:
"How do we recognize the suicidal person?"

5 ▶ Clues to Suicide: Prevention

The word *prevention* comes from the Latin *praevenire* meaning "to come before," "to anticipate." An awareness of the social and psychological antecedents of suicide may help us to understand and *prevent* human unhappiness.

"Why did he use his power and intelligence to destroy that power and intelligence?" This is the question asked by almost everyone who knows a suicide victim.

Sociologists see self-destruction as a barometer of social tensions. *Psychologists* interpret it as a response to the various levels of personal pressure. All agree that suicide occurs when there appears to be no available path that will lead to a tolerable existence.

But not everyone who is cut off from community ties or faces a business failure becomes a suicide victim. There is no single reason why a person takes his or her life. The factors differ from individual to individual. There is no single causative factor in suicide.

"If only I had known that she was thinking of taking her life," the survivors bewail. "I had no indication that such a terrible thing might happen." Yet almost everyone who seriously considers self-inflicted death offers some clues. Suicide does not occur suddenly, impulsively, un-predictably, or inevitably. It is the final step of a progressive failure at adaptation.

Among would-be suicides, 70 to 75 percent indicate their intentions in one way or another. Sometimes it is a subtle intimation; often the threat is unmistakably direct. Significantly, three-fourths of those who take their lives visit their physician on one pretext or another within months of the act. They seek an opportunity to speak out and to be heard. Too often both professionals and family just do not listen.

Suicidal people generally have ambivalent feelings. They may experience hopelessness but at the same time hope to be rescued. Often the factors for and against suicide are so evenly balanced that if those close to them responded in a warm, concerned, and knowing way, the scales could be tipped in favor of life. This is why it is so important to be aware of the clues and warnings that are communicated by the suicidal person.

▶ The Suicide Attempt

A history of a prior suicide attempt is a potent predictor of a subsequent completed suicide. For the surest sign of intent is the attempt. There is no more dramatic and poignant cry for help.

Some suicide attempts may not appear to be very se-rious. A young woman takes a bottle of pills at a time when she is sure to be discovered. Or a man purposely injures himself in a way that is not likely to be lethal. When an attempt of this nature is made, it is very easy for family and friends to ignore it or pass over it lightly. Even the individual who lightly overdosed may glibly try to explain it away. Too often people will dismiss the incident with the exasperated comment, "She was only trying to get attention." But *every* suicide attempt should be taken with the greatest serious-ness, no matter how harmless or frivolous as it may seem.

Those persons who are most vulnerable and at highest risk are those who have attempted suicide in the past, or have had close relationships with others who have tried or succeeded. Twelve percent of those who attempt suicide will make a second try and succeed within two years. Four out of five persons who do kill themselves have attempted to do so at least one time previously. After one abortive try, many resolve: "I'll do a better job next time." And they mean it, especially during periods of stress and turmoil.

▶ The Suicide Threat

The old myth that "those who talk suicide are merely talking and will never do it" has been proved to be dangerously false. On the contrary, many people who take their lives did speak about it, and in so doing disclosed their intentions. Initially, the threat could be an unconscious appeal for protection and intervention. Later, if no one seems really concerned, the person may set the time and determine the method of self-execution.

Some suicidal people are clear in their communication of intention. There are direct statements: "I can't take it. I don't want to live any more. I'm going to kill myself." Often the clues are veiled and disguised: "You won't have to worry about me. I won't be a problem for you." "I want to go to sleep and never wake up." "Soon this pain will be over." "They'll be sorry when I'm gone." "I wonder where my father hides his gun." Whether they take the form of a frank statement or a subtle hint, these significant danger utterances should not be ignored.

Sometimes the indications are nonverbal. Preparations before suicide vary with the person's personality and circumstances. They often consist of what is generally referred to as "getting one's affairs in order." For one adult, this might mean preparing a will and reviewing insurance papers. For another, it might mean writing long-overdue letters and patching up bad feelings with relatives or neighbors. To the teenager, it might mean giving away personal possessions with sentimental value—jewelry, skis, records. Final preparations may be made very quickly, with the suicide following abruptly.

▶ The Situational Hint

Stressful circumstances may make people more vulnerable to suicide. Something is happening both *within* them and *around* them. In a crisis situation their entire survival is threatened and they lose all perspective and balance. Prospects for the future appear bleak and hopeless.

In San Francisco, the situational findings of suicide are representative of the United States. The most common participating factors, in order of frequency, are as follows:

1. Suicide risk is high in persons who have recently been diagnosed as having a progressive *illness* such as multiple sclerosis or AIDS. The progression of the disease is more important in terms of suicide risk than the severity of the disability. A quadraplegic who is in pain often adapts if the condition is stable. However, a disease that requires one to readapt continually creates greater stress; some patients resolve to commit suicide rather than allow the disease to proceed past a certain point.

2. *Economic distress* affects more than just the pocketbook. Of course there is the crucial problem of food, clothing, and shelter. But in addition the competence of those affected is called into question. They feel that they are failures and have made a botch of their lives. Their future is suddenly uncertain, and suicide is contemplated as a way out of the situational dilemma.

3. With the *death of a loved one,* life will never be the same. The familiar design of family life is disrupted. The potential suicide may have an unusually long and severe grief reaction. There may be a continued denial of reality even many months after the funeral, prolonged bodily distress, persistent panic, extended guilt, an unceasing ideal-

ization of the deceased, enduring apathy, or a sustained hostile reaction to both friends and family. They cannot face the loneliness and void in their life. Suicide may promise relief from their psychic pain or a way to be united with their loved one. Suicide may even serve as a punishment for imagined or real acts perpetrated against the deceased.

4. In many ways, *divorce* and *domestic difficulties* can be more difficult to handle than death. When a person has died, there is a physiological explanation: "He had cancer." Or the theological view: "The Lord giveth, the Lord taketh away." With divorce, physical and religious reasoning are of no avail. Particularly where children are involved, there are the practical questions of custody and support along with unconscious feelings of guilt, failure, and revenge. Domestic problems have a profound effect on both parent and child. Studies reveal that many people who eventually kill themselves are the products of marital separation.

Specific stressful situations, such as illness, economic distress, death, and domestic difficulties often overwhelm a person's defenses. Despair and helplessness result from life's crisis. The situational hint is conducive to a suicidal response.

▶ The Family Hint

To understand suicidal people, one must be aware of their family circumstances because they often mirror their family's emotional disturbances. The environmental situation could determine whether their potential for self-destruction becomes realized.

For example, an individual is perturbed, doesn't eat regularly, and seldom spends time with friends. But he is not the only one who is disquieted. The other members of the household may also be in the throes of despair. In a study of adolescents who had taken their lives, it was discovered that almost all of the victims' parents were themselves depressed and preoccupied with suicide.

Or the rest of the family might be inflamed with anger and resentment. To vent their spleen, they unconsciously select one member to become the object of their accumulated aggression. Unfortunately, the person chosen does not know how to cope with their malice, and cannot retaliate or respond appropriately. If the person finally decides to take his or her life, it is really an acting out of the antisocial impulses that are covertly present in the other family members.

There may be a crisis situation—death, divorce, or loss of employment. The family's reaction to this change is one of wild alarm. Someone must pay for the disruption of social relations. The most vulnerable is the family member who is the least belligerent and articulate. Over and over, the "scapegoat" is told that he or she is the "bad one" who is responsible for the "terrible mess." The person may even be held accountable for the death of a family member who died of natural causes. People may take their life in the sincere belief that they are protecting those whom they love most. As a matter of fact, the suicidogenic family may even believe that, through the bizarre behavior of self-execution, the household's real problem is now solved.

Suicide cannot be meaningfully studied unless it is related to the social setting of the person involved. The needs, goals, and strivings of the significant others must be taken into account. One must understand the emotional climate of the family as well as the suicidal individual.

▶ The Emotional Hint

Emotional symptoms provide some of the best clues to a possible danger of suicide. Any sudden change in a person's personality is always a perilous warning.

The majority of potential suicides suffer from depression. Depression often begins insidiously with feelings of apprehension and despondency. They may not even remember when it all began. All they know is that lately they have been feeling sad, blue, "down-in-the-dumps." The future looks bleak and they think that there is no way they can change it. They imagine that they suffer from cancer, insanity, or some other dread malady. As a matter of fact, they have been thinking a lot lately about death and dying.

Ordinary tasks become difficult to perform. "I just can't think clearly," they say. They have difficulty in making even the simplest kind of decision. They exhibit lassitude and a lack of energy. They are always so tired.

Decreased sexual activity may be a signal of depression and associated suicidal thoughts. The disturbed people may think that they are sterile or impotent. Intercourse is no longer pleasurable. Dr. Norman Tabachnick is convinced that sexual grievances may be a distinguishing feature of those bent on self-destruction. Investigation of such complaints reveal a depressive condition, which on deeper probing may prove to have suicidal concomitants. Sexuality represents a protection against suicide when it is part of a pleasant and satisfying total relationship with another person. It is a component of the intimacy and closeness of a meaningful interpersonal experience.

In summary, emotional disturbance may include:

- ▶ a loss of appetite or sudden overeating, insomnia or excessive sleeping over a period lasting at least several days
- ▶ frequent complaints about physical symptoms that are often related to emotions (such as stomachaches, headaches, constant fatigue, frequent drowsiness)
- ▶ unusual neglect of personal appearance
- ▶ persistent feelings of loneliness, worthlessness, guilt, or sadness
- ▶ prolonged boredom in their surroundings and with activities that had previously been enjoyed
- ▶ withdrawal and isolation from friends and family, becoming loners who are unable to give of themselves or to make a real commitment in a relationship

- ▶ difficulty in concentration with a decline in the quality of work
- ▶ preoccupation with themes of death
- ▶ a lack of planning for the future—"Why worry about it? I could be dead tomorrow."
- ▶ abrupt outbursts of anger, "jumping" at little things; instead of controlling their moods, their moods control them

Many are depressed, and suicide may appear to be a solution to their emotional pain and unhappiness. Consider Joan, a nineteen-year-old college freshman who committed suicide. Her parents, friends, and teachers were shocked and bewildered. "After all," they lamented, "she never even talked about taking her life. How could this happen?" Yet there were many overt emotional symptoms of her distress. She had been skipping meals for weeks. "I just haven't felt hungry," she said. Joan seemed suddenly to become lethargic, withdrawn, and fatigued. She stopped answering her phone. She complained that she couldn't concentrate enough to study and wouldn't be able to take her upcoming final exams. In art class, she painted a young woman sprawled on a bathroom floor, pills scattered about. Friends noticed that Joan was obsessed with death, especially with morbid jokes about dying. Through her words and actions, she clinically expressed the potential to kill herself.

▶ Behavioral Hints

Before Joan killed herself, she displayed a number of behavioral changes. She was beginning to drink more frequently from the whiskey bottle she had in her closet, especially when she felt tense. In addition, she began to experiment with drugs. She offered her roommate her favorite earrings and necklace. She left college one morning without telling anyone. When she did not return after several days, the police were notified. Her body was found shortly thereafter.

Again, the indicators of suicide vary with each age group. In young people, the strongest clue to a suicidal tendency is abuse of drugs and alcohol. About half of the youths who commit suicide used drugs prescribed for their parents. In middle-aged persons, it is the inability to face up to their life situation, which is often expressed in somatic illness. In aged persons, talk of "giving up" may indicate a preoccupation with suicide.

▶ Mental Illness

Depressive disorders continue to be among the most pervasive mental and emotional problems confronting our society. According to Dr. Calvin J. Frederick, former president of the American Association of Suicidology: "Depression always carries with it the possibility of suicide, which has increased markedly over the past two and one-half decades."

Ours has been called the "age of depression." A recent survey of the readers of *Medical Times* reveals that it is the third most frequent reason for patients' visits to the family doctor. Depression is more than a temporary mood when people may occasionally feel "sad," "blue," "despairing," "dejected," "despondent," or "sorrowful." It is often mistaken for other conditions such as vitamin deficiency, "low blood," change of life, exhaustion, and "low sugar." Depression is a complex clinical syndrome that is difficult to differentiate and identify.

Perhaps the best approach would be a description of the consequences of depression. The disorder is extremely pervasive, affecting the individual's emotions, thinking, motivation, and physical functioning, and therefore his or her behavior and social interactions. The depressed person experiences genuine suffering and impairment—physiologically, physically, and socially. At times, the syndrome can be incapacitating and interfere with normal functioning at home, on the job, and in social contacts. It often leads to loss of employment, or breakup of a marriage or other close relationships. For some, depression is fatal. A majority of those who take their lives suffer from depressive illness.

Many of the symptoms of suicidal feelings are similar to the signs and symptoms of the depressed individual. The major symptom is loss of pleasure, the inability to enjoy those things in life that previously brought a measure of happiness. There could be a "flattening" of effect or mood. The mental state seems dull, without strong emotion. Feelings of demoralization, hopelessness, guilt, self-blame, and irritability are common. Motor activity is markedly slowed, or in contrast is speeded up, with loud, rapid, and sometimes incessant speech, often filled with complaints, accusations, and appeals for help. A change of sleep pattern accompanied by lethargy and waves of fatigue is a frequent symptom of depression. Physical indicators of anxiety include palpitations, dry mouth, and excessive perspiration. There are inexplicable somatic disturbances, with vague complaints of headache, backache, or abdominal pain, without apparent cause. Invariably they feel unwanted, sinful, guilty, and worthless, which leads them to the conclusion that life is not worth living.

In order to rule out an organic cause for depression, it is a good idea to include neurological testing in the physical examination of any individual perceived to be depressed and/or suicidal. Studies of the psychobiology of depressed people have demonstrated the deficiency of one or two special chemicals that carry messages from one nerve ending to the next across the small gap between. They deliver the message to the next nerve, then jump back to the nerve they came from. When a deficiency of messengers occurs in the brain, the result is emotional depression.

Another interesting biological finding is the familial incidence of depression. First-degree relatives of those with a history of depression are more likely to have a depressive disorder than are individuals with no family history of this affective problem.

The psychological cause of depression syndromes often centers on loss; perhaps the loss of a friend or relative, health, or job. The reaction may occur on the anniversary of a loss, even when the individual is not consciously aware of the recurrent date.

The elderly are among the most vulnerable to depression and, unfortunately, such depression is often regarded as a manifestation of senility. They are the most likely in our society to have suffered loss of friends and family, loss of financial resources, loss of familiar places, loss of health, loss of a sense of belonging and usefulness. It is important to distinguish between depression and senility in the elderly, since depression usually can be corrected. Otherwise, unchecked depression and consequent deterioration can lead to a feeling of hopelessness and a desire to die.

With loss, it is normal to be not only depressed, but to be angry as well. When this anger cannot be expressed, it may be turned inward so that tension and frustration complicate the grief. Physiological and psychological explanations for depression are not mutually exclusive.

Depression does not necessarily mean that the person is suicidal and psychotic. The great majority of depressed people are in touch with reality, can care for themselves, and on the basis of their clinical symptoms are not committable to a mental hospital. At the time of the act, they may be desperate. But so are many "normal" people who do not take their lives.

There are three common patterns of mental illness. *Neurosis* is the name for unreasonable fear and excessive tensions and anxieties. A neurotic person is in touch with reality but lacks confidence, feels mistrustful, and is continually anxious. *Character* or *personality* problems are evidenced by defects of conscience, judgment, or relationships. These people are not psychotic but participate in antisocial acts without a sense of guilt. *Psychosis* is the name for mental orders which are more serious than neurosis. The individual psychotic *usually* cannot function well in most aspects of the real world; i.e., hold a job or have family responsibilities. Included in the area of psychosis is manic depression, with its extreme shifts in mood from agitation to depression, perhaps with suicidal thoughts. The most common type of psychosis is schizophrenia, which results in delusions and hallucinations: voices and visions, "a nightmare made real." In schizophrenia things change shape and meaning without explanation.

Among those who are psychotic (estimated at less than one-quarter of suicidal patients), the suicide rate among schizophrenics and manic depressives is disproportionately high. Psychotically depressed people often become suicidal either when entering or leaving a totally depressed state. Various studies report that schizophrenic patients account for 3 to 12 percent of suicides. Long-term follow-up studies indicate that the lifetime risk of suicide for schizophrenics is between 15 and 20 percent. Schizophrenics often commit suicide in despair over their perceived inability to control their destiny or because of distressing delusions and persistent hallucinations.

► Those Most Susceptible to Suicide

The following significant risk factors have been identified as clues to those with the greatest predisposition to suicide:

- ► previous suicide attempt(s)
- ► suicide threat—direct or veiled
- ► family history of suicide
- ► alcoholism
- ► chronic use of bromides, barbiturates, and/or hallucinogenic agents

- ► affective disorders, especially severe depression
- ► manic-depressive psychosis .
- ► schizophrenia with secondary depression
- ► chronic or terminal illness, e.g., AIDS
- ► bereavement, especially widowhood during the first year of the death of spouse
- ► marital difficulties such as separation, divorce
- ► financial stress—joblessness, bankruptcy, loss of farm

In addition, the following groups have been found to have a greater risk of suicide:

- ► youths with negative, interpersonal relationships, "loners," those who exhibit alcohol or drug abuse, academic decline, or dangerous, illegal, or assaultive behavior
- ► young blacks and Hispanics
- ► gay men and lesbians
- ► Native Americans, especially males, in their twenties and thirties
- ► prisoners
- ► Vietnam veterans
- ► physicians and other professionals at the peak of their careers who are substance abusers, overly self-critical of themselves, or who have suffered recent humiliation or tragic loss
- ► middle-aged people who are overwhelmed by the disparity between expected achievement as opposed to perceived actual accomplishments
- ► elderly sick and abandoned individuals

Professionals as well as family and friends must *beware* of oversimplification or jumping to conclusions. Because people may fall into specific categories does not mean that they are suicidal. Again, there is no single causative factor in suicide. Yet all hints must be taken seriously. We must be *aware* that a combination of distress signals manifested over a period of time must bear watching. A cry for help needs a response from a helping person who can intervene during their lonely crisis.

6 ▶ Helping the Potential Suicide: Intervention

The word *intervention* comes from the Latin *inter* (between) and *venire* (to come). Suicide intervention is "coming between," that is, preventing an act of self-destruction. It is a supportive confrontation with troubled people through a compassionate response to their socio-psychological, existential human crisis.

Fortunately, no one is 100 percent suicidal. Notes often reveal the following kind of mixed emotions: "Dear Blanche, I have to kill myself. I hate you. All my love, Ed." The most ardent death wish is ambivalent. Part of the person wants to live, part wants to die. A suicidal state of mind is temporary—suicidal feelings may come and recur, *but* they almost always go. This is the basis of suicide intervention. Much depends on the helper, who can serve as a lifesaving agent.

▶ The Attitude of the Helper

Suicide is ugly for onlookers, devastating for relatives, and harrowing even for those professionally involved. Thus the entire subject is often avoided, even when individuals threaten to take their own lives. Some just do not want to become entangled in the sordid predicament.

Indifference, however, is not the same as being impartial. On the contrary, an aloof and unfeeling attitude is communicated to the highly sensitive, troubled person. It only confirms the suspicion that no one truly cares.

▶ The Helper as Moralizer

Because of ancient religious and historical taboos, many people regard the suicidal person with bias and bigotry. When the suicide threat is made, their response is, "You can't do that! It's against God and the faith."

The potential suicide is already suffering from a heavy burden of punishing guilt feelings. A potential helper who speaks of suicide as immoral will not only block the possibility of further communication, but may advance the suicidal individual's present sense of discouragement and depression. For the suicidal person, self-destruction is not a theological issue; it is the result of unbearable emotional stress.

Since people with suicidal tendencies are overwhelmed by sadness, discouragement, and disillusionment, they may act in a hostile manner. Unfortunately, family and friends may react with reciprocal indignation and resort to seething emotional arguments which only provoke the disgruntled individuals to even greater fury. They may be more concerned with the depressed person's infantile behavior than with meeting the desperation on a more caring and supportive level. By losing their temper, a life may be lost.

Intervention can be a frightening process. How to begin?

▶ What You Can Do to Help

1. *Recognize the clues of suicide*

Suicide prevention requires not only the concern of a friend but an ability to recognize the signs of danger. Your understanding of the principles of suicide prevention and your willingness to apply this information may save someone's life. By sharing that knowledge with others, you might also break down some of the misconceptions and myths that have kept many suicides from being prevented.

Look for the danger signs: suicide threat, previous suicide attempts, mental depression, marked changes in behavior or personality, or preparation for final arrangements. Be aware of signs of helplessness and hopelessness and notice whether the person has become withdrawn and isolated from others. The more people who understand these indicators, the greater the chance that suicide will eventually be removed from the list of leading causes of death.

2. Believe it

Accept the possibility that the person may really be suicidal. Don't assume that she or he isn't the "type" or "really wouldn't do it." The temptation is to deny the possibility that someone you care about would take his or her life. But that's how thousands of people—of all ages and races and economic groups—commit suicide. And don't allow others to mislead you into ignoring a suicidal situation. If you believe someone is in danger of taking a life, act on your own judgment. The danger that you might be embarrassed by overreacting is nothing compared to the danger that someone might die because you failed to intervene.

3. Form a relationship

There are no cut-and-dried answers to the profound problem of suicide. But you can take a giant step forward by demonstrating an unshakable attitude of acceptance toward the troubled person. Much depends on the quality of this relationship. It should be a relationship not only of words, but of nonverbal empathy as well; this is not a time for moralizing, but for loving support.

Instead of being chastised, the disquieted person should be put at ease and made to feel understood. To one who feels unworthy and unloved, caring and concern are great sources of encouragement. This way, you are more likely to pierce the harassed individual's prison of isolation.

4. *Be a good listener*

Suicidal people characteristically suffer from strong feelings of alienation. They may not be in a mood for your words of advice. They need to ventilate their own feelings of anguish and frustration and "I have nothing to live for." When individuals are depressed, they need to speak, not just to be spoken to.

You may feel frustrated, hurt, and even angry when the person doesn't immediately respond to your thoughts and needs. To know that someone you care about is feeling suicidal usually produces in the listener the feeling of being rejected, unwanted, powerless, or unneeded. Just know that at this time the other person has trouble concentrating on anything but his or her own unhappiness. They want to get away from their pain and just don't know a way out.

If they confide in you that they are contemplating suicide, do not condemn them for expressing their feelings. Try to be as calm and understanding as possible. You might say: "It takes a lot of courage to share your feelings and I appreciate your honesty." You can help by listening to their words and emotional reactions—whether they are sad, guilt-ridden, fearful, or angry. Sometimes just being with them without saying anything shows how much you care.

Professional and nonprofessionals alike should cultivate the art of "listening with a third ear." This means to concentrate on what is "said" through nonverbal manifestations: behavior, appetite, changing moods and outlook, agitated motor behavior, irregular sleep pattern, and impulsiveness in the face of an acute situational problem. Major precursors to suicide are often communicated in various disguised ways and may be detected by the perceptive listener.

5. Don't argue

Friends and family confronted by a suicide threat often respond with something like: "Think how much better off you are than most people; you should be thankful for how fortunate you are." That ends the discussion; it makes the person, who already feels miserable, even more depressed. Instead of being helpful, it is counterproductive.

Another familiar line is: "Do you realize the pain and embarrassment you'll cause your family?" This may be precisely the kind of revenge the suicidal person wishes to accomplish.

Do not react aggressively when you receive a suicidal communication and try not to be shocked by anything the person tells you. In the debate with the downcast person, you may lose not only the argument but also the individual.

6. Ask questions

Indirect questions like, "You're *not* thinking of committing suicide, are you?" indicate the answer you may want to hear. When the expected response is, "No, I'm not," you have failed to help resolve the individual's suicidal crisis.

The best intervention is to inquire *directly* and caringly: "Are you thinking of committing suicide?" Asking will not put the idea into his or her head. Rather, if the person is thinking about committing suicide, he or she will finally have found someone who cares and is willing to talk about this "taboo" subject. The individual is often relieved and able to begin an exploration of feelings and to engage is some catharsis.

Ask both calmly and clearly about the situation, for example, "How long have you felt that your life was so hopeless?" "Why do you think you are feeling that way?" "Do you have specific ideas about how you would kill yourself?" "If you thought about killing yourself before, what stopped you?" To help the people think through their thoughts, you might occasionally rephrase important responses: "In other words, what you are saying is that . . ."

Your willingness to share can be a relief to the troubled person, who probably feared that you would be judgmental and leave.

7. Do not give false reassurances

A psychological defense takes the form of rationalization. In response to a definite suicide threat, you might be tempted to say, "You don't really mean that." This evaluation may have no basis in fact whatsoever except in your own anxiety.

The reason that the individual is making the suicidal communication is to invite your concern about the state of his or her life. If you do not show that you care, the depressed person may perceive the statement "You don't really mean that" as a rejection and a lack of trust. People are *not* driven to suicide by loving inquiry. They may well be driven to self-destruction by platitudes when they desperately need a concerned and honest response.

Suicidal people detest statements such as "It's nothing—all people have problems just like yours" and other clichés that do not address the torment they are experiencing. This approach only belittles their feelings and makes them feel even more worthless.

8. Suggest positive approaches

Instead of demanding of suicidal people, "Think of how your death could hurt others," ask them to think of some alternatives that they have not examined.

One of the most important tasks in suicide intervention is to help identify the source of the distress. This may be difficult, since suicide thrives on secrecy. Relevant questions, to stimulate discussion, include: "What has been happening to you lately?" "When did you begin to feel worse?" "What is new in your life situation?" "What persons have been involved?" The potential suicide should be encouraged to diagnose the problem in their own words and to identify as precisely as possible the precipitating stresses.

The troubled individuals should be assured that they can express their true feelings with impunity. This includes negative emotions of hate, bitterness, and even a desire for revenge. If they are reluctant to share their innermost emotions, you may be able to evoke a response by observing: "You seem to be quite sad," or "You appear to be ready to cry." Or by stating: "You seem so troubled. Perhaps if you told me how you feel, I might understand."

The present emergency may be a disintegrating relationship with spouse and children. It may be unresolved grief. There may be an organic disease. Keep the feelings and troubles in view.

Once the crisis is more clearly identified and the venting of emotions has taken place, the next step is to clarify how the person handled similar situations in the past. This process is referred to as making an "inventory of problem-solving resources." One listens for references to experiences in the person's past which are analogous to the current scene. You might ask: "Does this remind you of the way you felt before?" Together, you may uncover the coping methods which had worked previously and may be useful in the present emergency.

Try to discover what still matters to them. What do they still value? Watch for signs of animation when the "best things" are touched on (noting especially their eyes). What is still available that has meaning? Who are those persons that continue to touch their life? Now that their life's situation has been reexamined, are there no alternative solutions? Is there not some ray of hope?

9. *Dare to hope*

Working with depressed people who are bent on self-destruction is an awesome responsibility. Yet psychotherapists have long recognized the value of giving full attention to what the distraught person is saying and feeling. When hidden thoughts are able to be expressed, troubles may seem less complicated and more solvable. The anxiety-ridden individual may even think: "I don't know the solution. But now that I have brought my difficulties out in the open, maybe there is some slight hope after all."

Hope helps to move a person out of suicidal preoccupation. Evidence of this can be seen in the behavior of the Jews during the nightmare of Hitler's concerted effort to annihilate them. In the years just before 1940, the average number of suicides in Holland for the month of May was 71.2. In May 1940, immediately after the Nazi invasion, there were 371. People took their own lives in anticipation of being sent to the dread concentration camps.

Initially the Jews who were interned retained some kind of faith in victory, with the confidence that families would soon be reunited. There were relatively few suicides in the camps as long as a shred of hope remained. When the conflict came to seem endless and news of the German slaughter of millions reached the inmates, the number of suicides grew to epidemic proportions. Still another wave took place at the end of the war when the former inmates discovered that their loved ones were dead and the full appalling horror of their death-camp experience was realized.

Suicide notes reveal the loss of hope and the seeming impossibility of a meaningful future. Self-destruction follows when people no longer have any measure of optimism and when this sense of futility is somehow confirmed by those close to them. Someone once said: "We make fun of people who hope and we put people in hospitals who do not."

Hope, however, must be based on reality. It is of little use to say, "Don't worry, everything will be all right," when everything will *not* be all right. Hope does not consist of false reassurances.

Hope springs not from fantasy but from the capacity both to wish and to achieve. A loved one who has died cannot be brought back to life no matter how much one hopes and prays. Yet survivors may discover some new meaning in life, even though part of them has died. If a ship founders on the rocks there is a difference between hoping to swim to the near shore and hoping to reach the other side of the ocean.

When people lose all hope for any kind of meaningful future, they may need the booster shot of having someone suggest alternatives. "What changes can you make?" "What pressures can you say 'no' to?" "Is there anyone you can turn to?"

Of course, since those who are suicidal suffer inner distress, everything may look totally bleak. But they may discover that they need not be stuck at one end of the spectrum. They can love without denying that sometimes they feel honest hate; life can still have some purpose even in pain. Darkness and light, joy and sorrow, success and suffering—all of these are inseparable strands in the texture of existence. The basis of a realistic hope must be communicated in an honest, convincing, and gentle manner. Emphasize the person's strength and the fact that while problems are usually temporary, suicide is permanent.

10. *Evaluate the seriousness of the suicide risk*

In addition to offering your support and a sense of hope, try to determine the immediacy of the danger of self-destruction. The person's intentions could range from fleeting, vague thoughts about "maybe thinking about it," or the plan could be more serious, involving drug overdose, shooting, hanging, poisoning, or jumping. Are there other factors such as alcoholism, drug abuse, high levels of stress and disorganization, and feelings of hopelessness and being out of control?

The more specific the method of self-execution, the higher the risk of suicide. There can be little doubt of the gravity of the situation when, for example, a depressed youth conspicuously gives away his stereo. Pills, guns, or knives should immediately be removed for safekeeping.

11. *Don't leave the suicidal person alone in a high-risk situation*

Stay with the person or ask someone else to stay with him or her until the crisis passes or until help arrives. It may be necessary to call a hospital emergency room or outpatient clinic. Relationships carry responsibilities.

You might involve the person in a *suicide contract*. That means asking the person to promise that she or he will contact you prior to attempting suicide in the future so that the two of you can discuss available alternatives. It may sound strange, but it can be very effective.

12. *Get help*

Suicidal people have a limited focus, a kind of "tunnel vision." Their mind does not always present them with the complete picture of how to handle their intolerable problems. Their first requirement may be for help in getting help. Friends may mean well but they may lack expertise and experience, besides being emotionally involved.

A possible helper is the clergy. William James thought of suicide as a "religious disease," the cure for which is "religious faith." Many ministers are superb pastoral counselors—understanding, sensitive, and supportive. But there are others who are untrained in crisis intervention. By moralizing and pious platitudes, they may push the parishioner into further isolation and self-recrimination.

Family physicians are also reliable resources. They usually know the intimate background of the patient and would be most helpful in both evaluation and referrals. Meanwhile, they might suggest some effective antidepressant drug to tide the person over until help is available.

The assistance of psychiatrists or clinical psychologists should never be underestimated. And, contrary to popular belief, mental health care is not just a luxury of the affluent. There are private as well as public agencies supported by national, state, and county funds which offer a wide range of services at low cost. By virtue of their knowledge, skills, and attitudes, therapists have a disciplined capacity to understand an individual's innermost feelings, demands, and expectations. Troubled people may be better able to reveal their profound anguish and anxieties during a psychotherapeutic consultation.

If the depressed person is uncooperative and will not seek help, another method of treatment is family therapy. Then the troubled individual isn't identified as "the patient." Everyone gets some support, and concerns and grievances are aired while all members of the family work out a way to live more comfortably and effectively together. Environmental changes may be suggested along with constructive plans to ease the tension and lessen the discomfort.

Sometimes hospitalization in a mental health facility may be the only alternative when the situation is desperate. Delay at this point can be dangerous; hospitalization can even prove to be a relief to both the patient and the family. Hospitals, however, are not always a panacea. Suicide may occur when the person is allowed to go home from the institution on leave, or shortly after discharge, or even during hospitalization. A study entitled "Predicting Post-Release Risk among Hospitalized Suicide Attempters" found that a significant factor is the attempters' definition of their situation at the institution. Do they see the hospital as a "prison" in which they are incarcerated? Those who define the mental hospital negatively at the times of admission and release are the highest suicide risks.

The study of hospitalized suicide attempters also concluded that those most prone to self-destruction view their crises in specific, personalized terms rather than as a general, diffuse condition. They react to perceived problems with violent, angry thoughts against their "significant others," later turning their fury against themselves as partial retaliation. They look upon their families as "negative others" because of a continued failure in communication. Following their release from the hospital, it was found that high-risk cases make poor social adjustments in the community. Some do in fact end their lives; others reattempt suicide and are again institutionalized.

13. *The importance of continuing care and concern*

Once the initial emergency is past, no one—professional or family member—can relax completely. The worst may *not* be over. Improvement is often confused with the person's increase of psychomotor energy.

Just prior to suicide, many depressed people rush into a welter of activity. They contritely apologize to anyone whom they think they have offended. Too often you breathe a sigh of relief and let down your guard. This phase may reflect only an inner resolve to wipe the slate clean. Now they can do away with themselves. And indeed, half the individuals who do commit suicide do so within ninety days after the precipitating crisis.

Sometimes forgotten in the tumult are the individuals who attempt to take their life. Ironically enough, many regard the people who attempt suicide and survive as failures. They earn the double contempt of being so "deranged" that they want to die and so "incompetent" that they couldn't even do the job properly. These people encounter great difficulty in finding acceptance and compassion in the family and in the community.

The emotional problems that led to the suicidal crisis are seldom fully resolved even when the worst has seemingly passed. That is why you should never promise total confidentiality. You are not performing a service by keeping silent. By signaling suicidal clues, the troubled person is asking for help. The emergency is never over until the would-be suicide is at home with life.

7 ▶ *When Suicide Is Committed: Postvention*

The word postvention comes from the Latin *post* meaning "after," "subsequent," or "later," and the Latin word *venire* (to come). The term postvention was introduced in 1971 by Dr. Edwin S. Schneidman for the purpose of understanding and assisting the family and friends *after* the death of a loved one who had committed suicide. Suicide leaves in its wake "survivor-victims." These survivors have indeed become victims. They have lost, as Schneidman notes, "their inalienable right to lead an unstigmatized life." He adds: "Studies show that survivors are apt to have a higher morbidity and mortality rate in the year following the death of their loved one than comparable persons who are not survivors of such death."

The death of any loved one can be devastating. However, the bereaved may find consolation in believing that it was God's will or in accepting the reality that there are simply limits to one's mortal existence. How much more traumatic when loss of life is self-willed! Where do the survivor-victims find consolation then? Suicide is the cruelest death of all for those who remain.

The "unpardonable sin" has been committed: the universal taboo, with its theological imprimatur, has been degradingly violated. Some say piously: "Suicide is self-murder. It is against the Sixth Commandment and the worst crime of all." Inwardly they may hold the family and close friends partially or wholly accountable for the "transgression."

For relatives and friends, intolerable feelings of guilt and grief remain. The widowed spouse will never know if some act of unkindness on his or her part was the spark that inflamed the mate with the desire to die. Parents feel that they must have failed their child miserably and blame themselves for their negligence. And the children of a suicide go through life haunted by the fact that they perhaps did something to cause the parent's death. They may even believe that the cruel seed that destroyed their mother or father is lurking in themselves as well, that something is wrong with their "psychological inheritance." There is for most suicide survivors the persistent, gnawing question, "What did I do wrong?"

▶ The Grieving Process

The goals in ministering to the family of the suicide are similar to those in helping all who face bereavement. In Erich Lindemann's words: "Grief work is emancipation from the bondage to the deceased, readjustment to the environment in which the deceased is missing, and the formation of new relationships."

But in comforting the bereaved, one must take into account the *special kind of death*. There are many survivor-victims. The immediate family members typically bear the brunt of the social stigma, and respond with deepened grief because of the blame placed on them by the community and by other family members themselves. Parents and siblings find it agonizing to bear the responsibility for such a death.

The pain of this terrible loss is also experienced by extended family members through the death of a grandchild, cousin, or in-law, often more keenly than kinship lines would seemingly indicate. Friends of the deceased may well find themselves with serious emotional reactions relating to the struggles that led their companion to take his or her life. Counselors and therapists may also be considered survivor-victims when one of their clients commits suicide—they may be seen as having failed to be a "competent" caregiver. Members of congregations, schools, workplaces, or churches/synagogues are demoralized that one of their own could take a life. The suddenness of loss could preclude a working through of emotions. Deliberateness of purpose in suicidal death intensifies the feelings of involvement in survivor-victims.

The only cure for grief is to grieve. There is no getting around the pain that a loved one willfully took his or her life. Grief is an emotion, not a disease. It's as natural as crying when you are hurt, eating when you are hungry, and sleeping when you are weary. Grief is nature's way of healing a broken heart.

No one can tell you how to grieve. There is no *normal* time span during which healing takes place. Some may vehemently protest that the terrible death has occurred; others may quietly resign themselves to the reality. Some may refuse to think about the death at all; others may think of nothing else. Some may cry hysterically; others may remain outwardly impassive and emotionless. Some may blame themselves for the death; others may project the guilt upon God, the physician, the nurse, the clergy, a friend, or even another member of the family. The grief process is never the same for any two people. Don't compare yourself with others in similar situations. Their smiles may not reveal the depth of their sorrow. Be your own timekeeper. Heal in your own way and in your own time. Each person's grief is different when coping with a suicide loss.

▶ Accept Your Grief

Allow yourself and those around you to feel the emotions that are a normal response to being so seriously wounded. "Keeping your chin up" only misleads you and others into a false sense of security.

In the beginning you may be in *shock*. You are bewildered, literally stunned. "I feel like a spectator in a play. But the drama is about me and the person I loved who took his/her life." You may feel numb all over, almost paralyzed in a world of unreality. Shock is a kind of insulation, cushioning you from the impact of this horrible, unexpected death.

You don't want to believe it. "It's a bad dream. When I wake up, I'll find it really didn't happen." *Denial* is when you secretly think or pretend your loved one will return and life will go on as before. It is so strange. You feel as if the suicide did not really occur, even though you *know* it really has. Many people need time before they can face the harsh truth. It is so hard to realize that in your lifetime you will never see or touch your loved one again.

There is *shame* and *embarrassment*. In addition to the cultural stigma placed on suicide, you may be subjected to investigations by police, coroners, and insurance agents. A woman about to be married asked: "Should I tell my boyfriend that my brother shot himself. I once told him that he was killed in a car accident. Maybe he'll think that my family is crazy and won't marry me."

You may think you are *losing your mind*. You want to run away—anywhere. You go over and over the event in your mind, imagining what your loved one experienced when he or she took the life. You are drawn to the obituaries, reading of people of the same age who also committed suicide. You may hurt so much that you want to die, too. "Wouldn't it be easier to join my loved one in death than go through the pain of living with this agony?" Just know you are *not* crazy. It takes time and effort to regain your ability to function more effectively.

Anger can be acute. It may be self-directed: "Why wasn't I at home when she took her life? Maybe I could have saved her." Resentment can be aimed at the counseling community: "Why didn't they prevent it?" Or the hostility could be leveled against the person who committed suicide: "How dare he do this to me and ruin my life?"

Emotional suffering following suicide often brings *physical distress*. Inside your chest you may feel a sharp pain as if a jagged rock is pressed against your ribs. You collapse in bed but cannot sleep through the long and torturous nights. Food may have little taste for you. You eat only because you think you should. Or else you just cannot stop eating. Your stomach may be tied in knots. Your back may be hurting. The pain is not imagined. It is real. Your body is feeling your agonizing emotional loss.

One of the most powerful reactions to loss through suicide is *guilt*. "I should have been there . . . offered more help . . . found the right solution. If only I had, s/he wouldn't be dead now." Few survivor-victims escape without a feeling of self-reproach. Suicide clues are often "discovered" after the death and you chastise yourself for not having discerned their meaning earlier.

Survivor-victims are often obsessed by the thought that they should have prevented the death, and see themselves as failures in the role of intervenor. Guilt may take the form of self-recrimination, depression, or hostility. There is a tendency to look for a scapegoat, often one who is least able to bear the added burden. There may be a direct accusation: "You killed him! You allowed it to happen!" Inwardly you may blame yourself but you turn the anger outward in the attempt to cope with your own guilt. Minor omissions come to mind and loom as major, significant causes of death. Again and again, you replay the event, devising actions that might have preserved the life.

Suicide often occurs when relationships break down. Before the death there may have been conflict and isolation in the family because of alcoholism, drug abuse, or antisocial acts. Guilt—real or imagined—is a prime aspect of suicide bereavement.

Relief is a commonly observed response to suicide loss. "Thank God, the suffering is over." Perhaps with death you are spared further anxiety about the continuing torment experienced by your loved one. Accept this relief and don't allow it to grow into inappropriate guilt. Remember, too, that the person who committed suicide considered death at that particular moment as the only possible alternative. Relief doesn't mean that you didn't love sufficiently or that you are callous, unfeeling, or selfish.

Especially in a case of suicide, you need to pour out your heart. What Sigmund Freud calls the "ties of dissolution" are extremely important and therapeutic at this time, that is, sharing both pleasant and unpleasant memories of the person who took his or her life. When each event is reviewed, a pang is felt at the thought that the experience will never again be repeated. As pain is felt, you begin to slowly loosen your emotional ties to the dead person. A gradual working over of old thoughts and feelings is a necessary part of the mourning process and a prelude to the acceptance of the suicidal death as a real fact with normal grief reactions.

Pathological grief

Among the many factors that can cause distorted mourning reactions is untimely loss by suicide. A death for which one is so completely unprepared has a more devastating impact than the loss of life from a chronic disease.

When grief work is not done, survivor-victims may suffer morbid distress characterized by delayed and pathological reactions. You may show great fortitude at the funeral but later develop symptoms of agitated depression and bodily affliction. You may complain of psychosomatic diseases such as ulcerative colitis, rheumatoid arthritis, asthma, and hypochondriasis (imaginary ills). Symptoms of a tension headache may lead you to conclude that you have a brain tumor; arthritic pain is interpreted as heart disease; constipation becomes a symptom of a malignancy. Obsessive-compulsive behavior may manifest itself. You may try to assuage your guilt through extreme cleanliness, or you may be unwilling to terminate the atmosphere of the funeral service by saying, "Tell me the eulogy again." There may be self-destructive behavior that is detrimental to your social and economic existence.

In general, one is able to distinguish normal from pathological grief not because the latter is abnormal or unusual per se, but rather because its reaction is so intensive and prolonged that it, in turn, jeopardizes your continuing physical and mental well-being. If you have any doubts about your emotional health, you should consult professional help. The period immediately following a suicidal death is a very precarious one in which repressed wishes, forgotten memories, and contradictory thoughts can run riot under the stress of shock.

▶ When to Seek Professional Help

There are dangers in prolonged depression and loneliness when:

- ▶ you continually feel hostile toward people you once cared about
- ▶ you are uninterested in anything and everyone
- ▶ your health is suffering markedly
- ▶ you are relying more and more on drugs and/or alcohol
- ▶ you avoid all social activities, wishing to be alone most of the time

▶ you, yourself, are preoccupied with thoughts of suicide

It is important to express your feelings with someone trained in grief counseling. Seeking professional help is not a sign of weakness, but a courageous resolve to take charge of yourself.

▶ The Funeral

No matter how difficult the emotional situation, your loved one has died and must be buried. It is understandable that when you hear the shocking news, your first impulse is to hold the funeral as quickly and quietly as possible. After all, there may be an aura of shame and dishonor. As a result, a private service may be contemplated for the immediate family.

No matter how great the humiliation, you cannot hide from reality, nor can you run away from the pain. A private funeral seems to say that the family is unable to bear the disgrace before their friends and neighbors and therefore want to keep it "secret." Survivors overlook one important fact—that, when given the opportunity, friends *can* be of help with their supportive love.

The funeral offers an important opportunity to comfort the mourners. It is the rite of separation. The "bad dream" is real. The presence of the corpse actualizes the experience. The process of denial is transformed to the acceptance of reality.

In the eulogy, the clergy should avoid any reference to blasphemy. People who took their lives were still individuals with strengths as well as weaknesses. The positive aspects of their life should be mentioned so that others can recall the happy times together and the many ways in which life was enriched by this presence. One judges a person by an entire life, not by an isolated moment, momentous as it may be.

▶ Children Grieve, Too

A person is a person no matter how small, and needs help during this crisis. Francine Klagsburn writes: "Children of suicide have a higher than average rate of suicide, not because the tendency to suicide is biologically inherited, but because they grow up with a heritage of guilt, anger, and a sense of worthlessness."

Don't pretend that life is unchanged

One of the worst problems is youngsters' lack of understanding because of adult secrecy. Give them clear, correct facts about the suicide in a comprehensible, compassionate manner.

Let them see your grief

Especially with suicide, you may be too consumed with your own pain and fail to reach out to the children. Expressing your own emotions is natural to the tragic situation and can provide the child with a basis for expressing his or her own feelings. Anger, despair, and protest are as normal for the youngster as they are for you. Especially be aware of children's guilt feelings and assure them that the suicide was *not* their fault.

Encourage them to participate in the family sorrow

Children, too, need to express their emotions through the ceremonies of death—the wake, the funeral, the shivah, the interment, the visitation. Do not plan one big "tell-all" about the suicide, but maintain a continuing dialogue. Explain in advance the funeral arrangements and give the child permission to attend. Be sensitive to the age and level of understanding of each child.

Avoid fairy tales and half-truths

Distortions of reality can do lasting harm. Do not tell a youngster what he or she will later need to unlearn. Use simple and direct language. It is preferable to hear about the circumstances of the death from you rather than from a friend, neighbor, or newspaper account.

Notify your child's school or day-care center

An understanding teacher can offer extra support when informed of the crisis in the child's life and better understand the youngster's class behavior. Reactions may not only be verbal but may include listlessness; withdrawal; aggressive behavior; physical symptoms, e.g., headaches, stomachaches; constant crying; regression to immature behavior; and especially poor performance of their schoolwork.

Do not place unnecessary burdens upon the youngster

The living child does not replace the dead sibling. When a parent takes a life, the youngster does not suddenly become the "man" or "woman" of the house. Children should become encouraged to be with their friends and become reinvolved in their usual activities.

Talk about the person who died

The child needs to talk, not just to be talked to. Try to recall not only the sad moment of death but the happy times together. They may also need to share their memories not only with you but with trusted friends as well. However, you should be selective about discussing some of the intimate details of the suicide.

Discuss constructive ways of handling the tragedy of the death

Even if a family member takes a life, children have choices in handling a crisis. They are different from the one who died. Suicide does not have to be their way out as it was for the individual who killed himself or herself. Tell them that if they give themselves time, their pain will diminish and they will begin to heal. No matter how dark the clouds may now look, they should always hang on a little bit longer. The sun may not be far behind.

When words fail, touch

Attitude can be more important than words. Your physical assurance of love and support is the greatest gift to a grieving child.

▶ Recovering from Grief

As soon as you can, start dealing with the facts of the suicide. The longer you delay, the more difficult the road to recovery.

Accept your grief

Expect the physical and emotional consequences of the death of your loved one. Grief is the price you pay for love. Don't be afraid to say the word *suicide*. It may take time, but keep trying.

Express your feelings

Don't mask your despair. Cry when you have to; laugh when you can. Your emotional needs must not be ignored.

Monitor your health

Eat as well as you can, for your body needs nourishment after the physically grueling experience of your grief. Depression can also be lightened by biochemical changes through proper exercise. Put balance back into your life with work and relaxation. Have a complete checkup and tell the physician about the loss in your life. You have suffered enough. Do not cause further damage to yourself and those around you by neglecting your health.

Be patient with yourself

Your mind, body, and soul need time and energy to mend from this tragedy. Grief is like weeding a flower bed in the summer: you may have to do it over and over again until the seasons change.

Share the pain of your darkness with a friend or friends

Survivor-victims tend to become paranoid and believe that everyone is whispering evil thoughts about them or blaming them for the death. It's crucial that you don't withdraw from others. By remaining silent, you deny friends the opportunity to share your inner self, bringing on more isolation and loneliness for you.

Join a group of others who are grieving

Learning about the experiences of others who have gone through similar tragedies can offer invaluable insights into your own feelings, while also providing support, encouragement, and friendship.

You might seek solace from your religious faith

Even if you ask, "How could God allow this to happen?" sorrow can be a spiritual pilgrimage. Religion is something you may wish to use—not lose—during your bereavement. You may be able to find comfort in a wisdom that has nourished souls of humankind for untold generations. Just remember that grieving deeply is no more an indication of weak faith than of strong faith.

Help others

By devoting your energies to people and causes, you learn to better relate to others, face reality, become more independent, and let go of the past by living in the present.

Do what has to be done but delay major decisions

Begin with little things—a single chore that has to be accomplished. That can help restore your confidence. But wait (if you can) before deciding to immediately sell your house or change jobs. Thomas Carlyle said: "Our main business is not to see what lies dimly at a distance but to do what lies clearly at hand."

Determine to live again

Readjustment does not come overnight. Make a start to put the stars back into your sky. Hold on to hope and keep trying. Resolve to survive each new day and do your best.

▶ Helping Survivor-Victims

People begin to help the bereaved when they attend the funeral and/or visitation. Being there is an eloquent statement that though a loved one had taken his or her life, friends still remain. Survivor-victims need all the support they can get.

And even when the funeral service has ended, friends need to be there. The family can feel very alone in dealing with their fear, confusion, anger, and guilt. It is so important that they have understanding friends who are sensitive to the depth and complexities of their feelings.

What can friends bring? Their best self—neither prejudiced nor judgmental. They have not come to justify or to censure: they have come, with love undiminished, as friends.

Conversation should be natural. Interest should be genuine and sincere. One should not try too hard. Oversolicitation only engenders further suspicions and guilt reactions. A most important way to encourage grief work is by responsive listening and empathetic discernment to what the other is experiencing from his or her internal, agonizing frame of reference.

Clichés are not helpful. Unsure of what to say when someone has died, one may try to comfort the bereaved with well-intended words:

"You're doing so well."

"Others have lived through it."

"You have two other children."

"I know just how you feel."

"Be strong."

"You'll get over it."

"Time will take care of everything."

"You're young. You'll get married again."

Since suicide is a blow and an affront to humanity, one may try to defend the survivor-victim by saying that the suicidal person was "out of his or her mind." But to inform a grieving individual that a loved one was "crazy" does not lighten the burden. Nor is it the truth. To quote Schneidman, Faberow, and Litman: "The majority of persons who commit suicide are tormented and ambivalent; they may be neurotic or have a character disorder, but *they are not insane.*" Telling the family that the person was crazy does not add to their social status; it only brings the fear of inherited mental disease. Survivors may believe that they are cast in the same mold as the suicide. They constantly recall how they resembled the victim both physically and mentally. They may begin to worry: "I keep thinking that I am losing my mind. I may kill myself someday. My father did, and I am just like him."

One might say: "There is much we do not know about suicide but we do know there is a limit to the load any person can bear. At that moment, death appeared the only alternative to the troubled life. But the ways of those closest to us are not necessarily our own ways." Professionals and friends can give an assurance based on empirical studies: "This I can tell you: suicide is not inherited."

Don't try to comfort the survivors by saying, "It was probably an accident." The family needs to start dealing with the reality of the suicide. Or "she or he was probably on drugs or drunk and didn't know what was happening." It is simply not helpful to give incomplete or false reasons for a multifaceted problem. Unfortunately, the survivors may feel even more alone and misunderstood when clichés are offered. Instead of telling them how they should feel, let them explain the emotions they are experiencing.

Bereaved people need to express their emotions. They can be encouraged to talk when others say:

"What are you feeling?"

"Tell me what is happening with you."

"It must be very hard on you."

Friends should focus on where they are. Accept their moods, whether they reflect fear or rage or panic. Friends are not there to judge but to listen, and the survivor-victims often need to talk about their loved one for months and years—not for just a few days following the funeral. Healing is a *long, long* process. Feelings and attitudes change. Just because the bereaved may refuse to talk on one day doesn't mean they don't need to communicate the following day. Friends must be sensitive to the shifting of moods.

While it is important to be there when the survivors need to talk, they should never be forced to share their inner emotions. Friends might simply say, "If you feel like talking, I'd like to listen." But conversation is not *always* necessary. Just as friends need to accept the bereaved's expression of emotions, they must also accept their silence as well. Love understands love; it needs no words.

Friends, as well as the bereaved, may need an opportunity to acknowledge their loss. Crying is a means by which people acknowledge the death of a loved one and work their way out of despair. Tears are not evidence of weakness. Weeping can be a shared experience.

Friends can also laugh with the bereaved when they need to laugh—not with forced frivolity, but with the enjoyment of recounting humorous times with their loved one. Death does not put a ban on laughter.

When words are sometimes meaningless, touching can be a most comforting way of communication. A squeeze of the hand or an embrace can eloquently tell them how much you care.

Friends might write in a letter some remembrances about the person who died. The note might say, "I want to share my own personal thoughts because the person was so important to me." Intimate notes are often prized and kept for years and years. Survivor-victims are reminded not how the loved one died but by how he or she truly lived.

Special dates like holidays, birthdays, and anniversaries are especially difficult for the bereaved. It's not a choice of whether or not they will experience grief, but how they will manage the grief they feel. Friends could call them on that special day just to tell them that they are thinking of them.

Friends may wish to invite them to share the day with them. Understand that the bereaved may need to express their suffering; no one need pretend that life continues just as it did before the person took his or her life.

Tell them about support groups, the sources of help from organizations of people who have suffered a similar loss through suicide. People in similar situations often become second families to each other, reaching out of isolation to a meaningful support system.

Above all, friends need to continue to call and visit. Don't just ask, do!

Telephone.

Visit.

Drop by with food.

Take the children on outings.

Invite the family to your home.

Survivor-victims desperately need *continuing* love, support, and concern.

▶ Withdrawal and Return

Following the suicide, the family will often say: "I would like to escape and never come back." Some remain in the same home but have run away as effectively as if they had moved to a distant country. They withdraw into their own room, isolate themselves from their friends and environment, and dwell bitterly on their tormented state.

They may take refuge in alcohol or prescription drugs. The bereaved may feel that sedatives and hypnotics that had been prescribed for the deceased or for themselves for an earlier malady must be safe or else the physician would not have recommended them in the first place. Unfortunately, such a solution may alleviate an anguished hour or a sleepless night, but it leads to further withdrawal, loneliness, and even addiction.

Some, in a desperate search for distraction at any cost, seek to escape through frantic activity. This may involve a fanatic dedication to some political movement or a continuous round of breakfast, luncheon, cocktail, and dinner meetings, with successive telephone conversations of endless length in between. The temporary release of tension becomes abortive, for the bereaved soon grow weary from physical fatigue and disenchanted with pseudoinvolvements.

Said Edna St. Vincent Millay:

> Life goes on . . .
> I forget just why.

After the funeral, the survivors should take time to think through which activities can bring some degree of purpose. They should start slowly and move carefully with friends who are supportive and understanding. Self-recrimination may still be present, but the most meaningful way to relieve the guilt is by transforming any errors of the past into a loving memorial by more noble behavior in the future. The goal is to assimilate the experience of grief and grow because of and through it.

In Hebrew there is a word: *t'shuva*. It means "to return," and implies the opportunity for renewal, a fresh start, an ever new beginning. Past failures need not doom a person forever. The willingness to build the temple of tomorrow's dreams on the grave of yesterday's bitterness is the greatest evidence of the unquenchable spirit that fires the soul of humankind.

Sometimes, the loneliness and sadness may come back for no special reason. Friends should be prepared for this. But survivor-victims can and will survive, even though there will be days when they may not wish to. These feelings do not last forever. Suicide victims can't expect to forget, but with time they will be better able to cope.

8 ► *Euthanasia: Killing and Letting Die*

► Euthanasia: What It Is

Theologians, social scientists, and legislators have long discussed the moral issue of euthanasia: is it mercy or murder? The word *euthanasia* is a term much misunderstood and hence widely feared. What exactly does euthanasia mean? In Greek, the prefix *eu-* means "good"; the suffix *thanatos* means "death." So euthanasia means quite simply "a good death." (During the Nazi regime the meaning of the word was corrupted and became associated with genocide and legalized mass murder.)

In his book *The Making of a Surgeon*, Dr. William A. Nolen described one case of euthanasia involving a 25-year-old man who suffered massive brain damage as a result of a motorcycle accident. For three weeks the patient was kept "alive" through tube feeding and respirators. Dr. Nolen writes that he wanted to shut off the respirator and allow the patient to die. "But I didn't," he said. "Few doctors do. Instead I waited for, almost prayed for a complication. It makes the decision easier." The complication arose. The patient developed pneumonia. Dr. Nolen decided not to administer antibiotics, and three days later the patient died. This is an example of one kind of passive euthanasia.

Passive euthanasia consists in withdrawing extraordinary life-prolonging techniques such as intravenous feeding and resuscitation or in not initiating such treatment when a situation appears hopeless. With the tremendous advances in the medical sciences, it is now possible to sustain terminal patients far beyond the time they might ordinarily die.

According to the *Physician's Washington Report* (1983), the President's Commission for the Study of Ethical Problems in Medicine and Biomedical and Behavioral Research issued a report addressing the "right to die." The Commission stated that mentally competent patients should have the right to discontinue any therapy that maintains life but offers no possibility of cure or improvement. The decision should be left to a family member or other surrogate when patients are incompetent to make the decision; only as a last resort should the courts be used.

▶ The Living Will

In 1967, the Euthanasia Educational Council (250 West 57th Street, New York, New York 10019) published the Living Will on the premise that the right to die is as valid as the right to live. It reads:

> *To My Family, My Physician, My Clergyman, My Lawyer*
>
> If the time comes when I can no longer take part in decisions for my own future, let this statement stand as the testament of my wishes:
>
> If there is no reasonable expectation of my recovery from physical or mental disability,
> I, —————, request that I be allowed to die

and not be kept alive by artificial means or heroic
measures. Death is as much a reality as birth,
growth, maturity and old age—it is the one cer-
tainty. I do not fear death as much as I fear the
indignity of deterioration, dependence and hopeless pain. I ask that drugs be mercifully administered to me for terminal suffering even if they
hasten the moment of death.

This request is made after careful consideration. Although this document is not legally bind-
ing, you who care for me will, I hope, feel
morally bound to follow its mandate. I recognize
that it places a heavy burden of responsibility
upon you, and it is with the intention of sharing
that responsibility and of mitigating any feelings
of guilt that this statement is made.

The Living Will, a voluntary document, asserts the individual's right to die and serves its most useful purpose in
mitigating the guilt of physicians and family when everything is *not* done to prolong the dying process. As of 1987,
thirty-six states had enacted legislation to establish standards for living wills, but Congress has not yet acted on the
matter.

In August 1987, a study was conducted by the Office
of Technology Assessment, Congress's research arm, which
stated that severely or terminally ill patients are often left
out of decisions on whether to keep them alive through
respirators or other treatments. Before he died of Lou Geh-
rig's Disease, a degenerative nervous system disorder, former senator Jacob Javits urged Congress to set national
standards governing the writing of such advance directions.
Mr. Javits said that people should have the right to die with
dignity "if hope is gone." John W. Rowe, a Harvard ger-
ontologist who headed the advisory panel of the Office of
Technology Assessment, stated: "Decisions on how to act

in certain situations in which lives are threatened are often based on the physicians' fear of malpractice litigation."

The issue of the terminally ill has been eloquently summarized by Dr. Jeremiah A. Barondess in an editorial in *The Journal of the American Medical Association:*

> The emergence of the living will and its growth into a widespread movement . . . are manifestations of multiple medical and social forces converging on the process of dying. The most prominent of these is the capacity of modern biomedical technology to prolong key physiological functions, often for long periods, in persons in comatose or vegetative states, regardless of ultimate prognosis. There has been increasing public awareness of this technological power and also of its potential impact, both emotional and financial, on the patient and his family. Just as physicians have been forced to reformulate the criteria permitting death to be diagnosed under these circumstances, now focusing on the viability of the brain, many current and potential patients have begun to consider new and broader definitions of life, chiefly in terms of sentient, cognitive functioning.

▶ Passive Euthanasia

The decision to extend life by artificial or other unusual means in the face of what obviously appears to be a fatal illness is one of the physician's most difficult and lonely tasks. These dilemmas include such questions as who should decide whether to introduce heroic measures in the hope of prolonging life and who should decide to stop them and when, particularly in the case of a patient who is no longer able to make decisions. Should the decision rest with the next of kin, who may earnestly wish to end the ordeal and yet, fear the accompanying guilt? Should it be made by the doctors, who know that the patient is terminal but who fear that their colleagues and the nurses will think them negligent for not having "done everything?" And always there is the pervasive fear of damage suits and malpractice. Should the compassionate physician continue heroic measures when cessation of therapy would in fact be more merciful? Is the primary mission of medicine the relief of suffering rather than its prolongation?

Passive euthanasia is performed every day in every part of this continent. Few of the cases receive publicity, for physicians simply let "nature take its course." Yet there are those who oppose passive euthanasia and insist that doctors should do everything possible to sustain life regardless of prognosis. They cite instances where patients pronounced "incurable" have miraculously recovered. They maintain that "where there's life there's hope." When a parent, husband, wife, or loved one is terminally ill, the attitude is— at whatever cost of grief, pain, and financial burden—that everything must be done to sustain life. The individual who pulls the plug of the mechanical respirator is considered guilty of murder and the patient who allows this act is in reality committing suicide. (These are the views, it must be remembered, only of those who *oppose* passive euthanasia.)

▶ Active Euthanasia

If a physician decides not to prescribe or continue utilizing a respirator for a hopelessly ill person, the doctor, as indicated, is *passively* responding to the patient's impending death. *Active* euthanasia consists in administering increasing doses of pain-relieving drugs such as morphine until the dosage reaches a lethal level, or in injecting air into a patient's veins, thereby *actively* contributing to the person's death.

Some of those who believe in active euthanasia—sometimes called "the right to suicide"—quote Nietzsche: "There is a certain right by which we may deprive man of life, but none of which we may deprive him of death." Active euthansia is regarded by its proponents as an issue of personal freedom. Everyone has a moral right to decide to live or die. The decision to choose death is the final expression of the right to be free. If the most skilled doctors determine that there is no hope for a terminal patient, then the patient and/ or family justly can exercise the right to end life.

Psychiatrist Thomas Szasz has been an eloquent spokesperson for active euthanasia. He writes in *The Second Sin*, "He who does not accept and respect those who want to reject life does not truly respect life itself." Instead of using the term *suicide* Dr. Szasz refers to "death control." Professor Marvin Kohl uses the expression "beneficent euthanasia." He states: "to require that a person be kept alive against his will and to deny his pleas for merciful release after the dignity, beauty, promise, and meaning of life have vanished when he can only linger on in stages of agony or decay, is cruel and barbarous."

In 1980 the Hemlock Society was created to introduce legislation to permit doctors to help dying people commit suicide. Relatives could help the doctors, who would not have to fear prosecution, that the person in question "could die with dignity." The executive director of the society, Derek Humphrey, in his book *Jean's Way*, describes how he assisted his dying wife by bringing her drugs and putting them in a cup of coffee. His wife, Jean, inquired: "Is that it?" And Derek responded: "If you drink that cup of coffee, you'll die. We said goodbye and she drank the cup of coffee. She took her life . . . I helped her and I committed a crime in doing so." In 1987, there were 13,000 members of the Hemlock Society supporting the option of active, voluntary euthanasia for the terminally ill.

Many, including religionists of most denominations, sanction passive euthanasia. In 1957 Pope Pius XII said that with the consent of the dying person "it is permissable to use with moderation narcotics that will allay suffering but also cause a quicker death." The pope also said that he did not consider the use of respirators as obligatory "since this form of treatment goes beyond ordinary method."

▶ The Right to Suicide

There is strong opposition to active euthanasia. Legally, and for many moralists as well, there is a significant difference between *allowing a person to die* (passive) and *killing* (active). A distinction is made between the active, intentional termination of life on the one hand, and abandoning heroic means to prolong life on the other. The House of Delegates of the American Medical Association agrees:

> The cessation of the employment of extraordinary means to prolong the life of the body when there is irrefutable evidence that biological death is imminent is the decision of the patient and/or his family. . . . The intentional termination of the life for one human being by another—mercy killing—is contrary to the policy of the American Medical Association.

Dr. Herbert Hendin, a recipient of the Louis I. Dublin Award of the American Association of Suicidology, asks in his book *Suicide in America* whether there is a right to suicide." He concludes with a resounding no. He writes: "If suicidal people were to organize or recruit others to their point of view, as happens in Robert Louis Stevenson's story, *The Suicide Club*, society should be able to intervene." Writing in the *American Bar Association Journal*, R. E. Schulman, a psychologist and attorney, expresses the feelings of many: "No one in contemporary Western society would suggest that people be allowed to commit suicide as they please, without some attempt to intervene or prevent such suicide. Even if a person does not value his own life, Western society does value everyone's life." Both medical advances and public opinion are forcing legislators to wrestle with the thorny question of euthanasia—passive and active. And ultimately, many of us will face it in our own lives.

9 ▶ *A Summons for Community Action*

▶ Making Death Come Alive

"To everything there is a season and a time to every purpose under the heaven; a time to be born, and a time to die."
—*Ecclesiastes* 3:1

There is no doubt as to the inevitability of death—our season will come. Death is the only event concerning the whole psychobiological organism which, once birth has taken place, is predictable beyond dispute. No one can be unaware that life has but a limited span.

And yet the subject of death is the most significant taboo of our society. There is a vast conspiracy involved in hushing up the the new four-letter word: *dead*. Death has become the forbidden topic, replacing sex as an unseemly topic of discussion.

The French philosopher La Rochefoucald captured this denial when he affirmed: "Neither the sun nor death can be looked at with a steady eye." Death is disguised through euphemistic language. People don't die, they "pass on" or "pass away." They "perish." They "expire." They become "deceased."

Death is not only camouflaged; it is avoided. For many, the theme is an obscenity not to be discussed or even mentioned. There is a superstitious belief that if it is not talked about, it will simply disappear. Death itself will "pass away." This is what some social scientists call the "dying of death."

This was not always true. For many, death was considered an ordinary aspect of life. Because of the high mortality rate, death was a frequent visitor. In contrast, the average child born in America today can expect to live beyond seventy-four, fully twenty-nine years longer than he or she could have at the turn of the century. In the past, multitudes of adults and children died in the home of bacterial pneumonia, diphtheria, and poliomyelitis. With the advent of antibiotics, vaccines, and improved sanitation, the once lethal effects of these maladies have now been virtually eliminated. Because our ancestors were in constant contact with death, they were compelled to view it as a real and natural phenomenon.

A modern American experiences death in his or her immediate family only once in every twenty years. Usually the event takes place *not* in the home but away in the hospital. Since there is infrequent exposure, death is not viewed as a pervasive factor of life but as a rare, impersonal, virtually abnormal event. While many people in the past believed in a kind of resurrection and salvation, the present generation's dissolving beliefs and traditions have eroded the consolation of a spiritual and physical immortality.

In addition to the advances of medical science and changing religious philosophies, there are accompanying demographic alterations. Some may still recall the time when most grandparents, parents, and children lived in the same household or certainly not more than a few houses or streets away. But at present, with the accent on mobility, members of most families are separated by states and even continents. They are shielded from the ravages of sickness and impending death.

The aged, those most susceptible to death, are kept out of sight. Growing old has become institutionalized in contemporary society. Some old people are relegated to a retirement village or community of senior citizens or sometimes to a nursing home. There they may await death in the same manner as the leper did in antiquity. As the elderly voluntarily or involuntarily remove themselves from the intimate family circle, younger members have less and less opportunity to experience death in an immediate, visceral, physical sense, and many do not witness the natural process of growing old.

Twentieth-century humans are trying to remove death from life's reality with hopes that they may unravel this final elusive enigma. After all, they have substantial mastery over their physical environment. Space exploration and technological discovery are becoming prosaic and commonplace. They tend to view dying and death in a detached, super-scientistic fashion. In laboratories around the world, technologists have begun to unlock the secrets of the aging process—and each new discovery improves the prospect of prolonging the years of youthful vitality. If the major killers of adults—cancer and diseases of the heart, kidneys, and blood vessels—were eliminated completely, researchers estimate that perhaps another ten years would be added to adult life expectancy. Some gerontologists have asserted that one may live almost indefinitely. So people talk not about the death of real individuals but the death of disease through organ transplantation and hemodialysis. They seek to deny or mitigate death with the primitive belief that death may no longer be inevitable.

Only within the last few decades has the area of death and dying become a respectable concern for the health professional and the social scientist. Heretofore, the topic was limited to theological speculation, philosophical interpretation, and literary expression. Instead of pretending that mortality is not a basic condition of life, the theme of death should become part of the curricula in colleges, high schools, elementary grades, and adult forums. The denial of death is impossible to sustain in a world of war, violence, and potential nuclear devastation. With exploding space shuttles, assassination of important personalities witnessed in living color on television, and losses in our own families, death must be brought out of the closet.

▶ Making Suicide More Understandable

Just as natural death cannot be ignored, neither can self-imposed death. Suicide has been known in all times and committed by all manner of people, from Saul, Sappho, and Seneca to Virginia Woolf, Sylvia Plath, and Freddie Prinze. Whether completed or not, suicide involves the most severe emotional turmoil, social discord, and terrifying disruption of life. No task demands so much skill, understanding, empathy, and support as ministering to those downcast people who can no longer find purpose in life, or to the family who has experienced the loss of a loved one through self-inflicted death.

Dr. Karl Menninger states: "To the normal person, suicide seems too dreadful and senseless to be conceivable. There has never been a wide enough *campaign* against it, as there has been against less easily preventable forms of death. There is not enough organized *public interest* in it. . . . In many instances, it could have been prevented by some of the rest of us."

▶ The Suicide Prevention Center

There are organizations for muscular dystrophy, multiple sclerosis, epilepsy, cerebral palsy. Yet until relatively recently efforts to control the major problem of suicide have been negligible. After all, does not an individual who *wants* to kill him- or herself have a *right* to do so?

But studies in the last decade now demonstrate that people want to commit suicide for only a relatively brief period of their lives. The suicide prevention center has been established to afford the potential suicide an effective sanctuary until the destructive impulse had passed. These pioneering social institutions afford the troubled person a place to turn to when all else seems lost.

The origins of the prevention center stem from the year 1774 in England, when a Royal Humane Society was created in order to frustrate attempted suicides. It was not until 133 years later, in 1907, that the National-Save-a-Life League was established in New York City. Staffed by sensitive volunteers who were seriously concerned with the problem, it was started by a clergyperson, the Reverend Harry M. Warren, who happened to visit a suicidal patient shortly before she died. She had said that if only he had come and spoken before, she wouldn't have attempted to take her life. He originated this group (which still exists in an Episcopal Church Center building in lower Manhattan) to help those in crisis.

Another clergyperson, the Reverend Chad Varah, organized a group in England called the Samaritans. He said:

> Whenever I hear myself referred to as the
> founder of the Samaritans, I want to protest. I
> didn't found them. They found me. When I read
> in the summer of 1953, that there were three sui-
> cides a day in Greater London, in spite of our ex-
> tensive medical and social services, I thought
> something ought to be done about it. . . . A per-
> son who is in despair and tempted to take his
> own life needs a compassionate human being to
> whom he can say "Will you help me? Now?"

The first Samaritan branch in the United States was opened in 1974 in Boston under the direction of Monica Dickens, an experienced London branch volunteer. Overseas branches extend from Brazil to New Zealand, preventing suicide by befriending the troubled.

The suicide prevention movement received greater attention when the National Institute for Mental Health in 1966 established the Center for Studies of Suicide Prevention "to effect a reduction in the present rate of suicidal deaths and to do it in such a way as to demonstrate unequivocally that lives have been saved." Two clinical psychologists, Drs. Edwin S. Scheidman and Norman L. Faberow, formed the Suicide Prevention Center of Los Angeles, one of the most effective and sophisticated of resources, whose competent personnel include psychiatrists, psychologists, social workers, plus a large number of carefully selected volunteers. Since then, more than two hundred suicide prevention programs have been established. (A list may be found on pages 128–43 of the book.)

There are many variations in the organizational structure of suicide prevention agencies. One unifying factor is the emergency telephone service designed to provide help immediately. The workers must establish rapport with the people at risk and communicate in an informal and personal interaction that they can help relieve the stress by talking out their problems.

The worker evaluates the suicidal potential of the caller. If the individual is at the telephone with a gun in his or her hand, then speedy assistance is urgently required. Resources used for quick referrals could be a general hospital, a psychiatrist in private practice, an outpatient clinic, a social service agency, a clergyperson, or a physician. Police may be utilized in cases of clear and immediate emergency such as when a caller requires prompt medical attention. Some agencies believe the family to be the most valuable referral in times of crisis; others consider close friends to be more helpful. Once the suicide crisis has passed, the caller may be referred to a social service or psychiatric helper.

According to Irene Trowell, a registered nurse, an ideal program would consist of:

- ► twenty-four-hour availability for those seeking help
- ► an active outreach for the elderly population and high-risk groups
- ► identification and follow-up of suicide attempters
- ► emergency rescue services
- ► consultation services for people in the community
- ► community education emphasizing clues to potential suicide
- ► twenty-four-hour hospitalization or an outpatient service program
- ► a suicide halfway house that offers services similar to drug and alcohol programs
- ► a partial hospitalization program that allows patients to leave the hospital and work during the day and then to return at night
- ► emergency mental health services, including suicide prevention and crisis intervention
- ► outpatient services
- ► a program for immediate referral to physicians, lawyers, and social, financial, and other agencies

Other organized efforts at preventing suicide include emergency room psychiatric services in general hospitals, community mental health centers, mental health clinics, pastoral counseling centers, antisuicide bureaus, hot lines, and poison control centers. In their respective ways they offer valuable services both to individual suicidal people and to the general community.

► Help for Families of Suicide

When all else has failed, there should be help for the living victims. Those who are left behind following a suicide often feel implicated in ways not generally experienced following other forms of death. The fact that the person *chose* to die makes a significant difference. Survivor-victims may feel a sense of scandal or disgrace and abandonment by friends. And for *all* there is the dreadful, haunting question, *"Why?"*

In many cities and towns, there are self-help organizations for families and friends of suicides. These are not therapy groups in the sense that participants are understood to be mentally ill. Usually there are no psychologists or therapists present. Rather, these organizations are opportunities for individuals to come together around a common experience, to share their stories and feelings, and to gain the support such sharing can provide.

One group, Ray of Hope, in Columbus Junction, Iowa, states:

> Just as potential suicides need the opportunity to express their feelings in a supportive, empathetic nonjudgmental atmosphere, so do the bereaved need to relate to others in the same situation and in the same way.
>
> OUR AIMS are to:
> *View suicide* as a social, health and spiritual problem which can be treated.
> *Develop* the use of mutual support groups for aiding the entire family in suicide situations.
> *Help provide* comfort and support for the bereaved.
> *Bring together* the bereaved with "significant others" who are concerned about someone, so through sharing their experience and growth, they may gain insights into behavior patterns and interpersonal relationships.
> *Co-operate* with community health agencies in referring members to seek additional help if they desire, realizing that professional services and support groups supplement each other although

they function in different ways.
Conduct research into the normal and atypical grief
processes following suicide.
Present seminars called SUICIDE: BEFORE AND
AFTER, designed to inform gate-keepers (both
professionals and lay persons) of the psychological first-aid for dealing with suicide situations (rec-
ognizing clues, learning responses, understanding motives, dispelling myths, etc.); and in
understanding the grief process.

Another group of caring people who are experiencing
the pain of a loved one's suicide call themselves Safe Place
of Stamford, Connecticut. To encourage newcomers to come
they write:

TO YOU ON YOUR FIRST VISIT

TO

SAFE PLACE

We've been helped.
　　We want to help you.
We ask only that you not judge how others
grieve.

We see changes in ourselves and in others in the
course of time.

We know that you will find friendship and support at our once-a-month meetings.

Help is available to you in many ways through:
　　Airing your feelings—we need to talk about
　　it . . .
　　　　Listening to others do likewise . . .
　　Being able to phone another survivor, when
you're having a bad day . . .

Gaining strength through association with those who demonstrate that they can, and are, "surviving" . . .

As you slowly, positively, reconstruct your life, you will benefit from the greatest healer— the knowledge that you will eventually be helping others—who, in months to come, will be on

THEIR FIRST VISIT
TO A SAFE PLACE

What inspiring examples that a community is more than a collection of homes! By helping to create vital relationships, they open new vistas, stimulate constructive changes, and convey a sharing desire to promote health and wholeness.

There is considerable optimism for the future. Scientists are continually adding to their knowledge of how the brain works and improving medicines to treat mental illnesses. There is also an increasing willingness to talk about mental illness and suicide.

But there is much to be done. Education is the *most* valuable tool to help in this endeavor. There *must* be an increased public awareness of the severity of the problem to encourage the development of new prevention programs and to support research on intervention and postvention efforts. Professionals must be better trained to detect the early warning signals and to learn how to take more effective preventive action. Schools—public, private, and religious— should set up programs not only on the topic of suicide, but also on how all of us can better handle stress and depression. Seminars and conferences should be offered to people of all ages. Legislators should recognize these pressing needs on a broader state and national level. The public must be aroused. Society should establish mental health as a *priority* or else there will likely be many more mourners.

If suicide is described as the desire-to-die, then we must be provided with the will-to-live and with the tools to cope through difficult times, realizing that *each life is unique, special, and worth preserving.*

► Conclusion

Life and death come into the world together; the eyes and the sockets that hold them are created at the same moment. From the moment we are born we are old enough to die. Life and death are contained within each other, complete each other, and are understandable only in terms of each other. How to *die* means nothing less than how to *live*.

Going into the question of suicide means breaking open taboos. Suicide puts society, religion, and the community of souls *in extremis*. Self-destruction is the paradigm of the individual's independence from everyone else. This is the reason the law has labeled it "criminal" and religion has called it "sin."

But name-calling is of no avail. What is crucial is to understand those who cry for help and to support them in their hour of need in the most meaningful and constructive way.

We can all bring something to the moment of crisis. This is portrayed most poignantly in Thornton Wilder's *The Bridge of San Luis Rey*, when the bridge collapses and plunges the persons crossing it to their deaths. In the attempt to discover what it was in each person's life that brought him

123

or her to the ill-fated bridge of self-destruction, Wilder enunciated one certain truth: "There is a land of the living and a land of the dead and the bridge is love—the only survival, the only meaning." For it is the death of love that evokes the love death.

▶ *Appendix*

▶ For More Information

Listed below are significant agencies and organizations that provide general information in the field of suicide.

National Information and Referral Sources

*National Committee on Youth Suicide Prevention
666 5th Avenue, 13th Floor
New York, N.Y. 10103
(212) 957-9292

American Association of Suicidology
2459 S. Ash
Denver, Colo. 80222
(303) 692-0985

Suicide Research Unit
National Institute of Mental Health
5600 Fishers Lane, Room 10C26
Rockville, Md. 20857

Suicide Education and Information Center
723 14th St., N.W., #102
Calgary, Alberta
Canada T2N 2A4
(403) 283-3031

Youth Suicide National Center
1825 Eye Street, N.W., #400
Washington, D.C. 20006
(202) 429-2016

*United Way Information and Referral Service
87 Kilby Street
Boston, Mass. 02401
(617) 482-1454

Community Mental Health Centers

Community mental health centers, psychiatric hospitals, and public or private psychiatric clinics are not listed in this directory, but these are often very useful referral agencies and information sources. Consult your telephone directories to

*These agencies provide local referrals.

locate these services, or contact the following agency for information about the community mental health center in your area:

National Council of Community Mental Health Centers
6101 Montrose Road, Suite 360
Rockville, Md. 20852

▶ Suicide Prevention/Crisis Intervention Centers in the United States

ALABAMA

Crisis Center of Jefferson
County, Inc.
3600 Eighth Avenue, South
Birmingham, Ala. 35222
Telephone: (205) 323-7777

North Central Alabama
Crisis Call Center
304 Fourth Avenue, S.E.
Decatur, Ala. 35601
Telephone: (205) 355-8000

Muscle Shoals Mental
Health Center
635 W. College Street
Florence, Ala. 35630

ALASKA

Suicide Prevention and
Crisis Center
825 L Street
Anchorage, Alaska 99501
Telephone: (907) 277-0222

ARIZONA

Mental Health Services
Suicide Prevention Center
1825 E. Roosevelt
Phoenix, Ariz. 85006
Telephone: (602) 258-6301

Suicide Prevention/Crisis
Center
801 S. Prudence Road
Tucson, Ariz. 85710
Telephone: (602) 795-0123

CALIFORNIA

Marilyn Adams Suicide
Prevention Center of
Bakersfield, Inc.
800 Eleventh Street
Bakersfield, Calif. 93304
Telephone: (805) 325-1232

Suicide Prevention of Santa
Cruz County, Inc.
P.O. Box 36
Ben Lomond, Calif. 95005
Telephone: (408) 426-2342

Suicide Prevention of
Alameda County, Inc.
P.O. Box 9102
Berkeley, Calif. 94709
Telephone: (415) 849-2212;
(415) 537-1323

Suicide Prevention and
Crisis Center of San
Mateo County
1811 Trousdale Drive
Burlingame, Calif. 94010
Telephone: (415) 877-5600

Monterey County Suicide
Prevention Center
P.O. Box 3241
Carmel, Calif. 93921
Telephone: (408) 649-8008

Help Line, Inc.
P.O. Box 5658
China Lake, Calif. 93555
Telephone: (714) 446-5531

Suicide Prevention of Davis
618 Sunset Court
Davis, Calif. 95616
Telephone: (918) 756-5000

Crisis House
126 W. Main Street
El Cajon, Calif. 92021

Saddleback Valley "Help
Line"
El Toro, Calif. 92630
Telephone: (714) 830-2522

Help in Emotional Trouble
P.O. Box 468
Fresno, Calif. 93721
Telephone: (805) 485-1432

Hot Line—Garden Grove
c/o Garden Grove
Counseling Service
12345 Euclid Street
Garden Grove, Calif. 92640
Telephone: (714) 636-2424

New Hope 24 Hour
Counseling Service
1241 Lewis Street
Garden Grove, Calif. 92640
Telephone: (213) 639-4673

"Help Now" Line
2750 Bellflower Boulevard,
Suite 204
Long Beach, Calif. 90815
Telephone: (213) 435-7669

Help Line Contact Clinic
427 W. Fifth Street, Suite
500
Los Angeles, Calif. 90013
Telephone: (213) 620-0144

Los Angeles Free Clinic
115 N. Fairfax
Los Angeles, Calif. 90038
Telephone: (213) 935-9669

Suicide Prevention Center
1041 S. Menlo Avenue
Los Angeles, Calif. 90006
Telephone: (213) 386-5111

North Bay Suicide
  Prevention, Inc.
P.O. Box 2444
Napa, Calif. 94558
Telephone: (707) 643-2555

Suicide Prevention and
  Crisis Intervention Center
101 S. Manchester Avenue
Orange, Calif. 92668
Telephone: (714) 633-9393

Suicide Crisis Intervention
  Center
c/o Palm Springs Mental
  Health Clinic
1720 E. Vista Chino
Palm Springs, Calif. 92262
Telephone: (714) 346-9502;
  business telephone: (714)
  327-8426

Pasadena Mental Health
  Association
1815 N. Fair Oaks
Pasadena, Calif. 91103
Telephone: (213) 798-0907

Psychiatric Crisis Clinic
Sacramento Medical Center
  Emergency Area
2315 Stockton Boulevard
Sacramento, Calif. 95817
Telephone: (916) 454-5707

Suicide Prevention Service
  of Sacramento County,
  Inc.
P.O. Box 449
Sacramento, Calif. 95802
Telephone: (916) 481-2233

Marin Suicide Prevention
  Center
P.O. Box 792
San Anselmo, Calif. 94960
Telephone: (415) 454-4524

Suicide Prevention Service
1999 N. D Street
San Bernardino, Calif. 92405
Telephone: (714) 886-4880

Defy Counseling Line
2870 4th Avenue
San Diego, Calif. 92103
Telephone: (714) 236-3339

Help Center
5069 College Avenue
San Diego, Calif. 92115
Telephone: (714) 582-HELP

Suicide Prevention, Inc.
307 Twelfth Avenue
San Francisco, Calif. 94118
Telephone: (415) 321-1424

Center for Special Problems
2107 Van Ness Avenue
San Francisco, Calif. 94109
Telephone: (415) 558-4801

Suicide and Crisis Service
645 S. Bascom Avenue
San Jose, Calif. 95128
Telephone: (408) 287-2424

North Bay Suicide
Prevention
401 Amador Street
Vallejo, Calif. 94590
Telephone: (707) 643-2555

Suicide Prevention Service
c/o Mental Health
Association
35 Chrisman
Ventura, Calif. 93003
Telephone: (805) 648-2444

Suicide Prevention-Crisis
Intervention
P.O. Box 4852
Walnut Creek, Calif. 94596
Telephone: (415) 939-3232

COLORADO

Arapahoe Mental Health
Center
551 Lansing
Aurora, Colo. 80010
Telephone: (303) 761-0620

Suicide Referral Service
P.O. Box 4438
Colorado Springs, Colo.
80930
Telephone: (303) 471-4357

Emergency Psychiatric
Service
Colorado General Hospital
4200 E. Ninth Avenue
Denver, Colo. 80220
Telephone: (308) 394-8297

Emergency Room
Psychiatric Services
Denver General Hospital
W. Eighth Avenue and
Bannock
Denver, Colo. 80206
Telephone: (303) 244-6835

Suicide and Crisis Control
2459 S. Ash
Denver, Colo. 80222
Telephone: (303) 746-8485

Arapahoe Mental Health
Center
4857 S. Broadway
Englewood, Colo. 80110
Telephone: (303) 761-0620

Crisis Center and Suicide
Prevention Service
599 Thirty Road
Grand Junction, Colo. 81501
Telephone: (303) 242-0577

Suicide Prevention Center
401 Michigan
Pueblo, Colo. 81001
Director: Layton P. Zimmer
Telephone: (303) 544-1133

DELAWARE

Psychiatric Emergency
  Telephone Service
Sussex County Community
  Mental Health Center
Beebe Hospital of Sussex
  County
Lewes, Del. 19958
Telephone: (302) 856-6626

Psychiatric Emergency
  Service
2001 N. DuPont Parkway,
  Farnburst
New Castle, Del. 19720
Telephone: (302) 656-4428

DISTRICT OF COLUMBIA

American University
  Multiple Emergency
  Center
Mary Graydon Center,
  Room 316
Washington, D.C. 20016
Telephone: (202) 966-9511

Suicide Prevention and
  Emergency Mental Health
  Service
801 N. Capitol Street, N.E.
Washington, D.C. 20002
Telephone: (202) 629-5222

FLORIDA

Alachua County Crisis
  Center
606 S.W. 3d Avenue
Gainesville, Fla. 32601
Telephone: (904) 376-4444

Suicide Prevention Center
P.O. Box 6393
Jacksonville,, Fla. 32205
Telephone: (904) 384-6488

Personal Crisis Service
30 S.E. Eighth Street
Miami, Fla. 33131
Telephone: (305) 379-2611

We Care, Inc.
610 Mariposa
Orlando, Fla. 32801
Telephone: (305) 241-3329

Rockledge Crisis and
  Suicide Intervention
  Service
Brevard County Mental
  Health Center
1770 Cedar Street
Rockledge, Fla. 32955
Telephone: (305) 784-2433

Crisis Intervention of
  Sarasota
1605 S. Osprey Avenue
Sarasota, Fla. 33578
Telephone: (813) 959-6686

Adult Mental Health Clinic
Pinellas County
630 Sixth Avenue
St. Petersburg, Fla. 33711
Telephone: (813) 347-0392

Suicide and Crisis Center of
  Tampa
1723 W. Kennedy
  Boulevard, no. 103
Tampa, Fla. 33606
Telephone: (813) 253-3311

Crisis Line
707 Chillingworth Drive
West Palm Beach, Fla. 33401
Telephone (305) 848-8686

GEORGIA

Fulton County Emergency
  Mental Health Service
99 Butler Street, S.E.
Atlanta, Ga. 30303
Telephone: (404) 572-2626

DeKalb Emergency and
  Crisis Intervention
  Services
Central DeKalb Mental
  Health Center
500 Winn Way
Decatur, Ga. 30030
Telephone: (404) 292-1137

Carroll Crisis Intervention
  Center
201 Presbyterian Avenue
Carrollton, Ga. 30117
Telephone: (404) 834-3326

Help Line
1515 Bull Street
Savannah, Ga. 31401

HAWAII

Suicide and Crisis Center of
  Volunteer Information
  and Referral Service
200 N. Vineyard Boulevard
Room 603
Honolulu, Hawaii 96817
Telephone: (808) 521-4555

ILLINOIS

Call for Help-Intervention
  Center
7812 W. Main
Belleville, Ill. 62223
Telephone: (618) 397-0963

Champaign County Suicide
  Prevention and Crisis
  Service
1206 S. Randolph
Champaign, Ill. 61820
Emergency telephone: (217)
  359-4141

Crisis Intervention Program
4200 N. Oak Park Avenue
Chicago, Ill. 60634
Telephone: (312) 794-3609

Crisis Counseling Service
Jefferson County Mental
  Health Center
1300 Salem Road
Mt. Vernon, Ill. 62864
Telephone: (618) 242-1511

Call for Help
320 E. Armstrong Avenue
Peoria, Ill. 61603
Telephone: (309) 691-7373

Suicide Prevention Service
520 S. Fourth Street
Quincy, Ill. 62301
Telephone: (217) 222-1166

Open Line Service
114 E. Cherry Street
Watseka, Ill. 60970
Telephone: (815) 432-5111

INDIANA

Suicide Prevention Service-
  Marion County
  Association for Mental
  Health
1433 N. Meridian Street
Indianapolis, Ind. 46202
Telephone: (317) 632-7575

Suicide Prevention of St.
  Joseph County
532 S. Michigan Street
South Bend, Ind. 46601
Telephone: (219) 233-1221

IOWA

Lee County Mental Health
  Center
110 N. Eighth Street
Keokuk, Iowa 52632
Telephone: (219) 233-1221

KANSAS

Area Mental Health Center
156 Gardendale
Garden City, Kans. 67846
Telephone: (316) 276-7689

Suicide Prevention Center
250 N. Seventeenth
Kansas City, Kans. 66102
Telephone: (913) 371-7171

Can Help
P.O. Box 4253
Topeka, Kans. 66604
Telephone: (913) 235-3434

Suicide Prevention Service
1045 N. Minneapolis
Wichita, Kans. 67214
Telephone: (316) 268-8251

LOUISIANA

Baton Rouge Crisis
  Intervention Center
Student Health Service, LSU
Baton Rouge, La. 70803
Telephone: (504) 388-8222

Crisis Line
1528 Jackson Avenue
New Orleans, La. 70130
Telephone: (504) 523-2673

MAINE

Dial Help
The Counseling Center
43 Illinois Avenue
Bangor, Maine 04401
Telephone: (207) 947-0366

Bath-Brunswick Area
  Rescue, Inc.
159 Maine Street
Brunswick, Maine 04011
Telephone: (207) 443-3300

Rescue, Inc.
331 Cumberland Avenue
Portland, Maine 04101
Telephone: (207) 774-2767

MARYLAND

Crisis Intervention and
  Problem Solving Clinic of
  Sinai Hospital of
  Baltimore, Inc.
Belvedere Avenue at
  Greenspring
Baltimore, Md. 21215
Telephone: (301) 367-7800

MASSACHUSETTS

Rescue, Inc.
115 Southampton Street
Boston, Mass. 02118
Telephone: (617) 426-6600

Samaritans of Boston
355 Boylston
Boston, Mass. 02138
Telephone: (617) 247-0220

MICHIGAN

Call Someone Concerned
760 Riverside
Adrian, Mich. 49221
Telephone: (313) 263-6737

Community Service
  Center—Chelsea
776 S. Main Street
Chelsea, Mich. 48118
Telephone: (313) 475-2676

Suicide Prevention Center
1151 Taylor Avenue
Detroit, Mich. 48202
Telephone: (313) 875-5466

Suicide Prevention Crisis
  Intervention Service
Community Mental Health
  Clinic
Ottawa County Building,
  Room 114
Grand Haven, Mich. 49417
Telephone: (616) 842-4357

Suicide Prevention and
  Crisis Intervention Service
5 E. Eighth Street
Office 601
Holland, Mich. 49423
Telephone: (616) 396-4537

Downriver Guidance Clinic
Community Crisis Center
1619 Fort Street
Lincoln Park, Mich. 48146
Telephone: (313) 383-9000

Crisis Center
29200 Hoover Road
Warren, Mich. 48093
Telephone: (313) 758-6860

Ypsilanti Area Community
  Services
1637 Holmes Road
Ypsilanti, Mich. 48197
Telephone: (616) 485-0440

MINNESOTA

Contact Twin Cities
83 S. Twelfth Street
Minneapolis, Minn. 55403
Telephone: (612) 341-2212

Crisis Intervention Center
Hennepin County General
  Hospital
Minneapolis, Minn. 55415
Telephone: (612) 330-7777;
  (612) 330-7780

Emergency Social Service
413 Auditorium Street
St. Paul, Minn. 55102
Telephone: (612) 225-1515

MISSISSIPPI

Listening Post
P.O. Box 2072
Meridian, Miss. 39301
Telephone: (601) 693-1001

MISSOURI

St. Francis Community
  Mental Health Center
825 Goodhope
Cape Girardeau, Mo. 63701
Telephone: (314) 334-6400

Western Missouri Mental
  Health Center
Suicide Prevention Center
600 E. Twenty-second Street
Kansas City, Mo. 64108
Telephone: none

Crisis Intervention, Inc.
P.O. Box 582
Joplin, Mo. 64801
Telephone: (417) 781-2255

St. Joseph Suicide
  Prevention Service
St. Joseph State Hospital
St. Joseph, Mo. 64506
Telephone: (816) 232-1655

Life Crisis Services, Inc.
7438 Forsyth, Suite 210
St. Louis, Mo. 63105
Telephone: (314) 868-6300

MONTANA

Blackfeet Crisis Center
Blackfeet Reservation
Browning, Mont. 59417
Telephone: (406) 338-5525

Great Falls Crisis Center
P.O. Box 124
Great Falls, Mont. 59401
Telephone: (406) 453-6511

NEBRASKA

Omaha Personal Crisis
  Service
P.O. Box 1491
Omaha, Nebr. 68101
Telephone: (402) 342-6290

NEVADA

Suicide Prevention and
  Crisis Call Center
Room 206, Mack SS
  Building
University of Nevada
Reno, Nev. 89507
Telephone: (702) 323-6111

NEW HAMPSIRE

Central New Hampshire
  Community Health
  Services, Inc.
5 Market Lane
Concord, N.H. 03301
Telephone: (606) 228-1551

North County Community
  Services, Inc.
227 Main Street
Berlin, N.H. 03570
Telephone: (603) 752-7404

NEW JERSEY

Ancora Suicide Prevention
  Service
Ancora Psychiatric Hospital
Hammonton, N.J. 08037
Telephone: (201) 561-1234

Middlesex County-Crisis
  Intervention
37 Oakwood Avenue
Metuchen, N.J. 08840
Telephone: (201) 549-6000

Screening Crisis
  Intervention Program
1129 N. Woodlane Road
Mt. Holly, N.J. 08060
Telephone: (609) 764-1100

Crisis Referral and
  Information
232 E. Front Street
Plainfield, N.J. 07060
Telephone: (201) 561-4800

NEW MEXICO

Suicide Prevention and
  Crisis Center of
  Albuquerque, Inc.
P.O. Box 4511
Albuquerque, N.M. 87106
Telephone: (505) 265-7557

The Crisis Center
Box 3563
University Park Drive
Las Cruces, N.M. 88001
Telephone: (505) 524-9241

The Bridge Crisis
  Intervention Center
113 Bridge Street
Las Vegas, N.M. 87701
Telephone: (505) 425-6793

NEW YORK

Suicide Prevention Center
Kings County Hospital
  Center
606 Winthrop Street
Brooklyn, N.Y. 11203
Telephone: (212) 462-3222

Suicide Prevention and
  Crisis Service, Inc.
560 Main Street
Buffalo, N.Y. 14202
Telephone: (716) 854-1966

Lifeline
Nassau County Medical
  Center
2201 Hempstead Turnpike
East Meadow, N.Y. 11554
Telephone: (516) 538-3111

Suicide Prevention and
  Crisis Service
P.O. Box 312
Ithaca, N.Y. 14850
Telephone: (607) 272-1616

The Norman Vincent Peale
  Telephone Center
3 W. Twenty-ninth Street,
  Tenth Floor
New York, N.Y. 10001
Telephone: (212) 686-3061

National Save-a-Life League,
  Inc.
815 Second Avenue, Suite
  409
New York, N.Y. 10017
Telephone: (212) 736-6191

Niagara County Crisis
  Center
527 Buffalo Avenue
Niagara Falls, N.Y. 14302
Telephone: (716) 285-3515

24 Hour Mental Health
  Information and Crisis
  Phone Service
260 Crittenden Boulevard
Rochester, N.Y. 14620
Telephone: (716) 275-4445

Suicide Prevention Service
29 Sterling Avenue
White Plains, N.Y. 10606
Telephone: (914) 949-0121

NORTH CAROLINA

Suicide and Crisis Service of
  Alamance County, Inc.
P.O. Box 2573
Burlington, N.C. 27215
Telephone: (919) 227-6220

Crisis and Suicide Center
300 E. Main Street
Durham, N.C. 27701
Telephone: (919) 688-5504

Crisis Help and Suicide
  Prevention Service of
  Gaston County
508 W. Main Street
Gastonia, N.C. 28052
Telephone: (704) 867-6373

Crisis Control Center, Inc.
P.O. Box 735
Greensboro, N.C. 27402
Telephone: (919) 275-2852

Care
215 Mill Avenue
Jacksonville, N.C. 28542
Telephone: (919) 346-6292

Suicide and Crisis
   Intervention Service
Halifax County Mental
   Health
P.O. Box 577
Roanoke Rapids, N.C. 27870
Telephone: (919) 537-2909

Crisis and Suicide
   Intervention
P.O. Box Q
Sanford, N.C. 27330
Telephone: (919) 776-5431

NORTH DAKOTA

Suicide Prevention and
   Emergency Service
Ninth and Thayer
Bismarck, N.D. 58501
Telephone: (701) 255-4124

Suicide Prevention and
   Mental Health Center
700 First Ave., South
Fargo, N.D. 58102
Telephone: (701) 232-4357

Northeast Region Mental
   Health and Retardation
   Center
509 S. Third Street
Grand Forks, N.D. 58201
Telephone: (701) 772-7258

St. Joseph's Hospital Suicide
   Prevention Center
St. Joseph's Hospital
Minot, N.D. 58701
Telephone: (701) 838-5555

OHIO

Support, Inc.
1361 W. Market Street
Akron, Ohio 44313
Telephone: (216) 434-9144

Suicide Control Center
Ashtabula General Hospital
505 W. Forty-sixth Street
Ashtabula, Ohio 44004
Telephone: (216) 963-6111

Crisis Intervention/Suicide
   Prevention
Athens Mental Health
   Center
Athens, Ohio 45701
Telephone: (614) 592-3917

Suicide Prevention and
   Crisis Help Service
2421 Thirteenth Street,
   N.W.
Canton, Ohio 44708
Telephone: (216) 452-9811

Suicide Prevention
1515 E. Groad Street
Columbus, Ohio 43215
Telephone: (614) 221-5445

Suicide Prevention Service
1435 Cornell Drive
Dayton, Ohio 45406
Telephone: (513) 223-4777

Town Hall II-Helpline
225 E. College Street
Kent, Ohio 44240
Telephone: (216) 672-4357

Rescue, Inc.
One Stranahan Square
Toledo, Ohio 43624
Mrs. William Hook
Telephone: (419) 243-4251

Crisis Hotline
2845 Bell Street
Zanesville, Ohio 43701
Telephone: (614) 452-8403

OREGON

Crisis Service
127 N.E. Sixth Street
Corvallis, Oreg. 97330
Telephone: (503) 752-7030

Crisis Center
University of Oregon
Eugene, Oreg. 97403
Telephone: (503) 686-4488

PENNSYLVANIA

Lifeline
520 E. Broad Street
Bethlehem, Pa. 18018
Telephone: (215) 691-0660

Suicide Prevention Center
Room 430, City Hall Annex
Philadelphia, Pa. 19107
Telephone: (215) 686-4420

SOUTH CAROLINA

Crisis Intervention Service
Greenville Area Mental
  Health
715 Grove Road
Greenville, S.C. 29605

TENNESSEE

Crisis Intervention Service
Helen Ross McNabb Center
1520 Cherokee Trail
Knoxville, Tenn. 37920
Telephone: (615) 637-9711

Suicide Prevention Service
P.O. Box 4068
Memphis, Tenn. 38104
Telephone: (901) 274-7473

Crisis Intervention Center
2311 Ellston Place
Nashville, Tenn. 37203
Telephone: (615) 244-7444

TEXAS

Call For Help
P.O. Box 60
Abilene, Tex. 79604
Telephone: (915) 673-8211

Suicide Prevention/Crisis
  Service
Box 3044
Amarillo, Tex. 79106
Telephone: (806) 376-4251

Contact—Tarrant County
Box 6212
Arlington, Tex. 76011
Telephone: (817) 277-2233

Information and Crisis
  Center
2434 Guadalupe
Austin, Tex. 78705
Telephone: (512) 472-2411

Telephone Counseling and
  Referral Service
c/o Counseling Center
The University of Texas
P.O. Box 8119
Austin, Tex. 78712
Telephone: (512) 476-7073

Suicide Rescue, Inc.
5530 Bellaire Lane
Beaumont, Tex. 77706
Telephone: (713) 833-2311

Suicide Prevention/Crisis
  Intervention
418 W. Coolidge
Borger, Tex. 79007
Telephone: (806) 274-5389

Crisis Intervention Service
P.O. Box 3075
Corpus Christi, Tex. 78404
Telephone: (512) 883-6244

Suicide Prevention of
  Dallas, Inc.
P.O. Box 19651
Dallas, Tex. 75219
Telephone: (214) 521-5531

Denton Area Crisis Center
Flow Memorial Hospital
Room 243, 1310 Scripture
  Drive
Denton, Tex. 76201
Telephone: (817) 387-HELP

Help Line
P.O. Drawer 1108
Edinburgh, Tex. 78539
Telephone: (512) 383-5341

Crisis Intervention
730 E. Yandell
El Paso, Tex. 79902
Telephone: (915) 779-1800

Crisis Intervention Hotline
212 Burnett
Fort Worth, Tex. 76102
Telephone: (817) 336-3355

Crisis Hotline
P.O. Box 4123
Houston, Tex. 77014
Telephone: (713) 228-1501

Contact Lubbock, Inc.
P.O. Box 3334
Lubbock, Tex. 79410
Telephone: (806) 765-8393

Suicide Rescue, Inc.
812 W. Orange
Orange, Tex. 77630
Telephone: (713) 883-5521

Crisis Center
709 Cliffside
Richardson, Tex. 75080
Telephone: (214) 783-0008

Crisis Center
P.O. Box 28061
San Antonio, Tex. 78228
Telephone: (512) 732-2141

Crisis Helpline
Box 57545
Webster, Tex. 77598
Telephone: (713) 488-7222

Concern
P.O. Box 1945
Wichita Falls, Tex. 76301
Telephone: (817) 723-8231

UTAH

Crisis Intervention Service
156 Westminster Avenue
Salt Lake City, Utah 84115
Telephone: (801) 484-8761

VIRGINIA

Northern Virginia Hotline
P.O. Box 187
Arlington, Va. 22210
Telephone: (703) 527-4077

Suicide-Crisis Center, Inc.
3636 High Street
Portsmouth, Va. 23707
Telephone: (804) 399-6993

WASHINGTON

Crisis Clinic
3423 Sixth Street
Bremerton, Wash. 98310
Telephone: (206) 373-2402

Emotional Crisis Service
1801 E. Fourth
Olympia, Wa. 98501
Telephone: (206) 357-3681

Crisis Clinic
1530 Eastlake East
Seattle, Wa. 98102
Telephone: (206) 325-5550

Crisis Service
107 Division Street
Spokane, Wa. 99202
Telephone: (509) 838-3328

WEST VIRGINIA

Suicide Prevention Service
418 Morrison Building
815 Quarrier Street
Charleston, W.Va. 26301
Telephone: (304) 346-3332

Contact Huntington
520 Eleventh Street
Huntington, W.Va. 25705
Telephone: (304) 523-3448

WISCONSIN

Suicide Prevention Center
310 Chestnut Street
Eau Claire, Wis. 54701
Telephone: (715) 834-5522

Walworth County Mental
Health Center
P.O. Box 290
Elkhorn, Wis. 53121
Telephone: (414) 245-5011

Emergency Services Dane
County Mental Health
Center
31 S. Henry Street
Madison, Wis. 53703
Telephone: (608) 251-2345

Psychiatric Emergency
Services
8700 W. Wisconsin Ave.
Milwaukee, Wis. 53226
Telephone: (414) 258-2040

WYOMING

Help Line, Inc.
Cheyenne, Wy. 82001
Telephone: (307) 634-4469

CANADA

Suicide Distress Centre
Box 393
Station K
Toronto, M4P 2G7
Canada
Telephone: (416) 598-1121

▶ Bibliography

Alvarez, A. *The Savage God.* New York: Random House, 1979.

Andre, J. M. *Suicide Occurrence in an American Indian Community.* Washington, D.C.: United States Public Health Service, 1975.

Aquinas, Thomas. *Summa Theologiae.* 2a–2ae.

Aristotle. *Nichomachean Ethics.* 1138.

Augustine. *The City of God.*

Barrett, Tom. *Youth in Crisis.* Longmont, Colo.: Sopris West, 1985.

Beck, A. T., and M. Kovachs. "Alcoholism, Hopelessness, and Social Behavior." *Journal of Studies on Alcohol* 37 (1976).

Becker, Ernest. *The Denial of Death.* New York: Free Press, 1973.

Bell, Ruth, and Leni Zeiger Wildflower. *Talking with Your Teenager.* New York: Random House, 1983.

Blackstone, William. *Commentary on the Laws of England.* Vol. 14.

Blos, Peter. *The Young Adolescent.* New York: Free Press, 1970.

Bolton, Iris, and Curtis Mitchell. *My Son, My Son.* Atlanta: Bolton Press, 1983.

Breasted, J. H. *Ancient Records of Egypt.* Vol. 4. New York: Russell and Russell, 1972.

Bressler, B. "Suicide and Drug Abuse in the Medical Community." *Suicide and Life-Threatening Behavior* 6 (1976).

Brown, Norman. *Life against Death*. New York: Random House, 1959.

Busse, E. W., and E. Pfeiffer. *Mental Illness in Later Life*. Washington, D.C.: American Psychiatric Association, 1973.

Butler, R. N. "Psychiatry and the Elderly." *American Journal of Psychiatry* 132 (1979).

Cain, A. C., ed. *Survivors of Suicide*. Springfield, Ill.: Thomas, 1972.

Camus, Albert. *The Fall*. Translated by J. O'Brien. New York: Modern Library, 1964.

Charon, Jacques. *Suicide*. New York: Charles Scribner's Sons, 1972.

Cohn, E. P. *Suicide among the Elderly: The Religious Response*. In press.

Coleman, W. L. *Understanding Suicide*. Elgin, Ill.: David C. Cook, 1979.

Conte, H. R. "Personality and Background Characteristics of Suicidal Mental Patients." *Journal of Psychiatry* 10 (1974).

Douglas, Jack. *The Social Meanings of Suicide*. Princeton, N.J.: Princeton University Press, 1967.

Dublin, Louis. *Suicide: A Sociological and Statistical Study*. New York: Ronald Press, 1963.

———. *To Be or Not to Be*. New York: Harrison Smith, 1933.

Durkheim, Emile. *Suicide*. Glencoe, Ill.: The Free Press, 1972.

East, W. N. "On Attempted Suicide with an Analysis of 1,000 Consecutive Cases." *Journal Mental Science* 59 (1913).

Ellis, Edward. *Traitor Within: Our Suicide Problem*. Garden City, N.Y.: Doubleday, 1971.

Erikson, Erik. *Identity: Youth and Crisis*. New York: W. W. Norton, 1968.

Farber, Maurice. *Theory of Suicide*. New York: Funk and Wagnalls, 1968.

Faberow, Norman L. *Bibliography on Suicide and Suicide Prevention*. Washington, D.C.: Government Printing Office, 1970.

———. *The Many Faces of Suicide*. New York: McGraw-Hill, 1980.

———. *Taboo Subjects*. New York: Atherton Press, 1966.

Faberow, Norman L., and E. S. Schneidman. *The Cry for Help*. New York: McGraw-Hill, 1961.

Feifel, Herman, ed. *The Meaning of Death.* New York: McGraw-Hill, 1959.

―――. *New Meanings of Death.* New York: McGraw-Hill, 1977.

Frederick, Calvin J., and Louise Lague. *Dealing with the Crisis of Suicide.* Public Affairs Pamphlet no. 406A. Public Affairs Commission, 1972.

Freud, Anna. *The Ego and the Mechanisms of Defense.* New York: International Universities Press, 1971.

Freud, Sigmund. *Mourning as Melancholia.* London: Hogarth Press, 1957.

Friedman, Paul. *On Suicide: With Particular Reference to Suicide among Young Students.* New York: International Universities Press, 1967.

Fulton, Robert, ed. *Death and Dying.* Reading, Mass.: Addison-Wesley, 1978.

―――. *Death and Identity.* Bowie, Md.: Charles Press, 1976.

Gallagher, J. R., and H. I. Harris. *Emotional Problems of Adolescence.* New York: Oxford University Press, 1976.

Giovacchini, Peter L. *The Urge to Die: Why Young People Commit Suicide.* New York: Macmillan, 1981.

Gordon, Sol. *When Living Hurts.* New York: Union of American Hebrew Congregations, 1985.

Griffin, Mary, and Carol Felsenthal. *A Cry for Help.* Garden City, N.Y.: Doubleday, 1983.

Grollman, Earl A. *Concerning Death: A Practical Guide for the Living.* Boston: Beacon Press, 1974.

―――. *Living When a Loved One Has Died.* Boston: Beacon Press, 1987.

―――. *Talking about Death: A Dialogue between Parent and Child.* Boston: Beacon Press, 1976.

―――. *Talking about Divorce and Separation: A Dialogue between Parent and Child.* Boston: Beacon Press, 1975.

―――. *Time Remembered: A Journal for Survivors.* Boston: Beacon Press, 1987.

―――. *What Helped Me When My Loved One Died.* Boston: Beacon Press, 1981.

Grollman, Earl A., and Sharon Grollman. *Caring for Your Aged Parents.* Boston: Beacon Press, 1978.

Guest, Judith. *Ordinary People.* New York: Viking, 1976.

Haim, André. *Adolescent Suicide*. New York: International Universities Press, 1975.

Hankoff, L. D., and Bernice Einsidler. *Suicide: Theory and Clinical Aspects*. Littleton, Mass.: P. S. G. Publishing, 1971.

Hatton, C. L., and S. M. Valente. *Suicide Assessment and Intervention*. Norwalk, Conn.: Appleton-Century-Crofts, 1984.

Hendin, Herbert. *Age of Sensation*. New York: W. W. Norton, 1975.

―――. *Black Suicide*. New York: Harper and Row, 1975.

―――. "The Psychodynamics of Suicide." *Journal of Nervous Mental Disorders* 136 (1963).

―――. *Suicide and Scandinavia*. New York: Grune and Stratton, 1964.

―――. *Suicide in America*. New York: Norton, 1982.

Henry, Andrew, and James Short. *Suicide and Homicide: Some Economic, Sociological, and Psychological Aspects of Aggression*. Glencoe, Ill.: Free Press, 1954.

Hewett, J. H. *After Suicide*. Philadelphia: Westminster Press, 1980.

Hillman, James. *Suicide and the Soul*. New York: Harper and Row, 1964.

Holinger, P., and D. Offer. "Prediction of Adolescent Suicide." *American Journal of Psychiatry* 139 (1982).

Horney, Karen. *Neurosis and Self-Growth*. New York: W. W. Norton, 1950.

Hume, David. *On Suicide*. Edinburgh: Black and Tait, 1826.

Jackson, Edgar. *For the Living*. Des Moines: Channel Press, 1963.

―――. *The Many Faces of Grief*. Nashville, Tenn.: Abingden Press, 1977.

―――. *Understanding Grief*. Nashville, Tenn.: Abingden Press, 1972.

Kalish, Richard A. *Death and Ethnicity*. Los Angeles: University of Southern California Press, 1976.

Kandel, D. B., and M. Davies. "Epidemiology of Depressive Mood in Adolescents." *Archives of General Psychiatry* 39 (1982).

Kastenbaum, Robert, and Ruth Aisenberg. *The Psychology of Death*. New York: Springer Publishing House, 1972.

Kiev, Ari. *The Courage to Live*. New York: Crowell, 1979.

————. *The Suicidal Patient.* Chicago: Nelson Hall Publishers, 1971.

Klagsbrun, Francine. *Too Young to Die: Youth and Suicide.* Boston: Houghton Mifflin, 1976.

Kohl, Marvin, ed. *Beneficent Euthanasia.* Buffalo: Prometheus Books, 1975.

Kübler-Ross, Elisabeth. *Death: The Final Stage of Growth.* New York: Prentice Hall, 1975.

————. *On Death and Dying.* New York: Macmillan, 1970.

————. *Questions and Answers on Death and Dying.* New York: Macmillan, 1974.

Lester, David. *Why People Kill Themselves.* 2d edition. Springfield, Ill.: Charles C. Thomas, 1983.

Lester, David, and M. E. Murrell. "The Preventative Effect of Strict Gun Controls on Suicide and Homicide." *Suicide and Life-Threatening Behavior* 12 (1982).

Lester, Gene. *Suicide: The Gamble with Death.* Englewood Cliffs, N.J.: Prentice-Hall, 1971.

Lindemann, Erich. "Symptomatology and Management of Acute Grief." *American Journal of Psychiatry* 101 (1944).

Linzer, Norman. *Suicide: The Will to Live vs. the Will to Die.* New York: Human Sciences Press, 1984.

Litman, Robert, and C. I. Wold. "Beyond Crisis Intervention." In *Suicidology in Contemporary Developments,* edited by E. S. Schneidman. New York: Grune and Stratton, 1971.

McCoy, Kathleen. *Coping with Teenage Depression.* New York: New American Library, 1982.

McIntire, Matilda, and Carol Angle. *Suicide Attempts in Children and Youth.* Boston: Harper and Row, 1980.

McIntosh, J. L. *Research in Suicide: A Bibliography.* Westport, Conn.: Greenwood Press, 1985. Bibliographic citations on suicide since 1970. Divided into ten chapters by subject.

Mack, John, and Holly Hickler. *Vivienne: The Life and Suicide of an Adolescent Girl.* New York: New American Library, 1982.

Madison, Winifred. *Portrait of Myself.* New York: Random House, 1979.

Maguire, Daniel. *Death by Choice.* New York: Schocker Books, 1975.

Marius, R. W. *Pathways to Suicide.* Baltimore, Md.: Johns Hopkins University Press, 1981.

May, Rollo. *Love and Will.* New York: W. W. Norton, 1969.

Menninger, Karl. *Love against Hate.* New York: Harcourt, Brace, 1952.

———. *Man against Himself.* New York: Harcourt, Brace, 1966.

Merloo, Joost. "Hidden Suicide" In, *Suicidal Behaviors,* edited by H. L. P. Resnick. Boston: Little, Brown, 1968.

———. *Suicide and Mass Suicide.* New York: Grune and Stratton, 1962.

Miller, Marv. "Suicide after Sixty." *Thanatos* 3 (1978).

Morrison, J. M. *Your Brother's Keeper.* Chicago: Nelson-Hall, 1981.

National Institute of Mental Health. *Bibliography on Suicide and Suicide Prevention.* Chevy Chase, Md.

Osherson, Samuel. *Holding On or Letting Go.* New York: Free Press, 1980.

Peck, Michael, Norman Faberow, and Robert Litman, eds. *Youth Suicide.* New York: Springer, 1985.

Phillips, D. P., and K. A. Bollen. "Imitative Suicides: A National Study of the Effects of Television News Stories." *American Sociological Review* 47 (1981).

Plato. *Phaedra.* 62b–c.

Portwood, Doris. *Common Sense Suicides: The Final Right.* New York: Dodd, Mead, 1978.

Rado, S. "Psychoanalysis of Pharmacothymia." *Psychoanalytic Quarterly* 2 (1933).

Resnik, H. L. P. *Suicidal Behaviors: Diagnosis and Management.* Boston: Little, Brown, 1968.

Resnik, H. L. P., and B. C. Hawthorne, eds. *Suicide Prevention in the Seventies.* Rockville, Md. NIMH Center for Studies of Suicide Prevention, 1973.

Ross, C. "Mobilizing Schools for Suicide Prevention." *Suicide and Life Threatening Behavior* 10 (1980).

Schneidman, Edwin S. *The Cry for Help.* New York: McGraw-Hill, 1961.

———. *The Definition of Suicide.* New York: Harper and Row, 1980.

———, ed. *Essays on Self-Destruction.* New York: Science House, 1967.

———. *Voices of Death.* New York: Harper and Row, 1980.

Schneidman, Edwin S., and N. L. Faberow, eds. *Clues to Suicide.*

New York: McGraw-Hill, 1957.

Spillard, A. *Grief after Suicide.* Pamphlet. Waukesha, Wis.: Mental Health Association of Waukesha County, Inc.

Stengel, E. *Suicide and Attempted Suicide.* Baltimore, Md.: Penguin, 1969.

Stone, Howard. *Suicide and Grief.* Philadelphia: Fortress Press, 1972.

Szasz, T. S. *The Myth of Mental Illness: Foundations of a Theory of Personal Conduct.* New York: Harper and Row, 1974.

———. *The Second Sin.* Garden City, N.Y.: Anchor Books, 1974.

Tabachnik, Norman D. *Accident or Suicide?* Springfield, Ill.: Thomas, 1973.

Topol, R. "Perceived Peer and Family Relationships: Hopelessness as Factors in Adolescent Suicide Attempts." *Suicide and Life Threatening Behavior* 12 (1982).

Ullman, L. P., and L. A. Krasner. *A Psychological Approach to Abnormal Behavior.* Englewood Cliffs, N.J.: Prentice-Hall, 1975.

Varah, Chad, ed. *The Samaritans.* New York: Macmillan, 1965.

Vaux, Kenneth L. *The Will to Live, the Will to Die.* Minneapolis: Augsburg Publishing House, 1978.

Wells, Carl, and Irving Stuart. *Self-Destructive Behavior in Children and Adolescents.* New York: Van Nostrand Reinholt, 1981.

Weisman, Avery. *On Dying and Denying: A Psychiatric Study of Terminality.* New York: Behavioral Publications, 1972.

———. *The Realization of Death.* New York: Jason Aronson, 1974.

Weisman, Avery, and J. W. Worden. "Risk-Rescue Rating in Suicide Assessment." *Archives of General Psychiatry* 26 (1972).

Winokur, G. *Depression: The Facts.* New York: Oxford University Press, 1980.

Worden, J. M., and W. Proctor. *Personal Death Awareness.* Englewood Cliffs, N.J.: Prentice-Hall, 1976.

Wrobleski, A. *Suicide Questions and Answers; Suicide: The Danger Signs; Suicide: Your Child Has Died—For All Parents.* Minneapolis, 1984.

———. *Afterwords: Letters about Suicide and Suicide Grief.* Minneapolis: Newsletter, 1987.